STANDARD BAKING CO.

PASTRIES

STANDARD BAKING CO.

PASTRIES

ALISON PRAY
TARA SMITH

Photography by
SEAN ALONZO HARRIS

Down East Books

To our wonderful customers and talented staff who have made the bakery what it is.

Copyright ©2012 by Alison Pray and Tara Smith

Design by Miroslaw Jurek
Photographs by Sean Alonzo Harris

Library of Congress Cataloging-in-Publication Data

Pray, Alison.
Standard Baking Co. pastries / by Alison Pray and Tara Smith.
p. cm.
ISBN 978-1-60893-184-2
1. Baking. 2. Bakeries. 3. Standard Baking Co. (Portland, Me.) I.
Smith, Tara. II. Title. III. Title: Pastries.
TX763.P683 2012
641.7'1--dc23
2012018990

Printed in China

Down East Books
www.nbnbooks.com
Distributed by
National Book Network
800-462-6420

CONTENTS

FOREWORD

Standard is a bakery without spin. You won't find art work on the walls, fancy coffee drinks or deli sandwiches. The bread and pastry sell themselves.

Standard isn't a brand, it's a philosophy. That Standard exists and thrives in a city like Portland speaks of the creative, entreprenurial, do-it-yourself spirit of its community. Portland is a community where good food is synonymous with good life. In such a community, Standard is a cornerstone to a morning routine, an evening meal, a celebration.

A visit to Standard Baking in winter is a feast of contrasts. Tourists are long gone. The streets are nearly empty and noiseless in new snow. Mornings arrive late and darkness comes early. Your only real outing this time of year may be your twice weekly walk to Standard in the morning. Outside is biting and bitter; inside, the bakery is a haven of moist warmth, steaming the windows. A dozen customers squeeze into the tiny vestibule, blowing into their unmittened hands or cradling cups of coffee, waiting their turn to order. No one is in a hurry. Smiles are exchanged and greetings passed. You may not know all their names but the faces of these customers are familiar. You've seen them manning retail shops, taking tickets on a ferry boat, driving a snow plow, or walking a dog on the street where you live. In the long winter months, this many people gathered in such a small space for the single pleasure of baked goods grounds you to this corner of Maine and makes you glad to live here. You tear into the heel of your still-warm baguette or flaky croissant as you walk out the door. It seems it was baked just for you. You can taste the care that went into its making. In a world set on rushing you through life, Standard Baking Co. reminds you to slow down, take time and care in all you do. As you head back out into the icy morning, you notice a gold slip of light over Casco Bay.

Jane Newkirk
Bath, Maine

MY JOURNEY AS A BAKER BEGAN WITH A TRIP TO FRANCE.

My husband, Matt James, and I fell in love with the French lifestyle, which revolves around fresh, wholesome food. Seeking out the day's groceries proved to be as rich an experience as visiting any museum. Open-air market tables overflowed with beautiful displays of local produce and artisanal foods. Cities and villages alike teemed with the most tempting charcuterie, cheeses, vegetables, fruits, and chocolates.

But what most captivated me were the boulangeries and patisseries. Deeply caramelized tarts filled with local apples, apricots, cherries, and plums seemed to glow in the shop windows. The stacks of crusty pavé loaves (named for their brick-like appearance) looked both irresistible and too elegant to eat. Children eagerly lead their mothers home, carrying fresh baguettes to be served with lunch. Baking was not simply a craft but an art built on timeless techniques, passed down through generations. Matt and I envisioned opening our own bakery in the French-style—a refuge in our fast-paced world. And I wanted to learn what the French bakers knew.

Over the next few years I studied with and worked alongside many talented bakers, read copiously, and experimented constantly. I discovered that as a baker, you can't rely on recipes alone, you come to count on your senses. You learn how to create a tender flaky pastry by handling the dough, time and again. Eventually, the sense of touch becomes your guide. Your sense of smell along with visual cues help you gauge when a pastry is ready to come out of the oven. I quickly learned that the success of even the best recipes depends on attention to details such as accurate measurements, precise temperatures, and exact pan placement in the oven.

In 1995, Matt and I opened Standard Baking Co. in a tiny storefront on a cobblestone alley.

Operating on a shoestring, we purchased a couple of used pizza ovens, built our bread racks from reclaimed pine floors, and installed a counter made from a beautiful slab of Carrara marble, salvaged from Portland City Hall. Before opening to the public, we spent months of painstaking experimentation, developing an authentic French baguette for the restaurant next door, doing all of our test baking in an ancient restaurant oven and tabletop toaster oven.

We imagined our small bakery as a place where everyone would feel comfortable stopping by for daily bread or morning pastry. The baked goods would be the attraction and reflect the care of the bakers who crafted them. We chose our name, Standard, feeling that it evoked a time and place when people relied on their local butchers, grocers, and bakers—and more than anything else, we hoped our neighbors would feel they could rely on us to provide their daily needs for wholesome breads and handmade pastries.

Five years later we moved to our current location—a historic warehouse on Portland's bustling waterfront . We now bake our breads in a twelve-ton masonry oven and prepare Viennoiserie and a myriad other confections in a temperature-controlled pastry room. The understated design of our bakery reflects our attitude towards baking and food in general—that good food should never feel artificial or contrived. Without any walls separating the baking area, our retail shop is filled with a constant hum of activity and anticipation.

Standard Baking embodies our belief that good food should reflect the essence of the ingredients. We strive to create baked goods that are fresh, delicious, unfussy, and appealing to the eye. Everything we make is from scratch with the intention that it will be eaten the same day.

Successful baking is based on sound technique. Although it is a science, it's less important to know the chemistry involved than it is to bake often, closely observing the transformation of the ingredients. To gain mastery, there is no substitute for repetition. You'll soon enough reach the point where you've become so familiar with a recipe that you can begin to make changes, noting the subtle differences that occur.

We are very pleased to pass on the tips and techniques we've learned over the years. There's something for everyone here, regardless of your baking experience. We hope we've conveyed our own sense of discovery and excitement about baking and that you'll have fun reproducing some of Standard's most popular items in your own home.

Alison

IF ONE WERE TO OBSERVE ME BAKING AT HOME,

it wouldn't be immediately obvious that I work in a bakery. How I bake in my home kitchen is very different from the way I bake at work. At the bakery I am precise, efficient, and my perfectionist tendencies are the driving force of my day. Unless I am creating a new item, every recipe must be followed exactly as written every single day. The objective is to create consistent, delicious pastries in staggering quantities for our hungry patrons. At home, I am free to relax the rules. I can linger over the mixing bowl, eat more dough than cookies, and make a total mess of my kitchen. I have been known to shove peanut butter cups and butterscotch chips into recipes for which they were never intended! I get a certain amount of pleasure plopping differently sized cookies on my baking sheet—I like when some are crunchy and others are soft and chewy. Baking at home allows me to indulge my guilty pleasure of taking an elegant recipe and making it homey and whimsical. Conversely, it also gives me a chance to dress up and elevate an old family favorite.

Particularly at home, a recipe is simply a jumping off point for me, and I rarely make a recipe the same way twice. I'm always thinking about what to try next. A different pan, new ingredients; whatever I can do to take ownership of the recipe and create something unique! So, the recipe is inspiration, and what follows is an expression of creativity and my fascination with the process. Experimentation is great fun—as long as you don't have great expectations for your first trial. There is a lot to learn throughout the process. You could stumble upon a brilliant new discovery in the world of pastry. If not, at least the failures are still often edible!

Baking is a science. The way that ingredients interact with each other and change in the depths of your oven is complicated. Although it is a science, remember that your kitchen is a far cry from a laboratory! In the best of circumstances, it's very difficult to control all the variables that can affect the outcome of a recipe. Flour moisture levels vary, humidity and room temperature change daily, the age and quality of ingredients—all these things and more can have an impact on the results of your baking endeavors. But don't let that scare you! Bakers have been doing wondrous things for millennia without knowing the science behind the process.

The best advice I can give? Pay attention to your results! Try to note any changes that occur each time you make a recipe. Knowing the science is great, but observation is just as important. You must learn to channel your inner grandmother, knowing instinctively when to throw in an extra handful of flour, a splash more milk, or when to leave your babka an extra hour to rise in a cool kitchen. Foster these instincts. Trust yourself to evaluate your results and make changes. Once you know the basics, you can bend the rules. I often get calls from family and friends in a panic because they want to make something and don't have the "required" pan or ingredient. In most cases, a substitution is easily found. The second best advice I can give? Don't be afraid to experiment. Give it a whirl and see what happens! And get to know your oven – chances are it has its own individual quirks and inconsistencies. When the cookies in the back right-hand corner are always burned, that might mean rotating a pan in your oven every 5 minutes, even though the recipe says every 10. Your own kitchen is a unique place, so make an effort to work with it.

As much as I enjoy being a casual home baker, there are lessons that I learned at culinary school and through my work experiences that I will never forget, and can apply to my efforts at work and at home. I had great teachers to start me on my way as a baker, and through their collective advice and guidance, I've gained the confidence to experiment, to trust my instincts, and to always remain open to learning. I endeavor to work efficiently, cleanly, and accurately, but am always striving for improvement. Over the years, I've also learned about what it really means to be a part of the large community working to provide good food for our families and patrons. Jeffrey Hamelman once told me (after I had made a huge error and ruined a day's worth of croissants) that when you are baking, you should seriously contemplate the ingredients that you are using. To paraphrase, he said, "Think about the wheat that was milled for your flour. Think of the farmer that tended it. Think of the miller that milled it. Think of the truck driver that brought it to you. Think of the cow that gave the milk that went into the butter, and the chicken that gave its eggs. How much energy went in to what you have in front of you? It is staggering to count how many hands have come together to create one simple croissant. Don't let them down!" I am honored to be the last link in this long chain. Bringing all of these wonderful ingredients together to create something that brings sustenance and happiness is a pleasure!

Tara

INGREDIENTS

The healthful properties of food are as important to us as taste and texture. Overly sweet, sugary baked goods are not part of the Standard repertoire. We prefer to use a variety of sweeteners such as honey and maple syrup, molasses, brown sugar, and minimally refined turbinado or Demerara sugars. We use real butter produced from naturally raised animals; local, organic eggs from humanely raised hens; whole nuts; organic fruits; fine sea salt; and local honey. The availability of these ingredients inspires us to create recipes that resonate with the bounty of the seasons.

When recipes are as uncomplicated as most of these are, the freshness of every ingredient is key to baking delicious pastries. We will always choose an organic ingredient if it's available and if it will work in our recipe. We anticipate the growing sources of local ingredients becoming more widely available to us, providing added inspiration when we develop new recipes each new season.

Butter

We always use unsalted butter for its pure flavor. When making croissant and other laminated doughs, where the fat to flour ratio is high, we use a higher butterfat content of around 83 percent, which has better spreading quality (referred to as plasticity) that helps to stabilize the butter layers in the dough. For both laminated and tart doughs, we like to use butter with the lowest water content, for the flakiest pastry. Ours comes from a Vermont creamery, but Plugrá is an excellent brand that is widely available.

Flour

All of our recipes use unbleached, all-purpose flour, unless otherwise noted. For slightly more tender tart doughs or scones, substitute a small portion of pastry flour, up to 25 percent of the total flour in the recipe, and reduce the liquid slightly. Unbaked tart dough won't hold together as easily, but you can just trim the edges and use those pieces to patch any tears. Measure flour carefully. These recipes were tested using the scoop and level method—scooping the flour out of the bag with a utensil into a measuring cup, leveling the excess with a straight edge.

Chocolate

In the bakery we use Callebaut bittersweet and unsweetened chocolate slabs. We use chunks of bittersweet chocolate in our chocolate chip cookies and other pastries. Cocoa colors and flavors vary widely and will affect the results of your baking. We chose ours from Cacao Barry, a Belgian chocolate maker, for it's well-balanced flavor. It is Dutch-processed, very dark in color, and gives our baked goods a deep brown-black hue that we like.

Eggs

It is more than worth the effort of seeking out local, farm fresh eggs. Compared to conventional store bought varieties, the whites will be firmer, the yolks a deep orange that will give your cakes a warm, golden crumb. We source our eggs only from local, organic farms because we believe that the use of synthetic chemicals in food harms our bodies and our environment, and because sustainable farming is only possible if we support our local farmers. We call for large eggs in all of these recipes.

BREAKFAST PASTRIES

The pace is brisk in the morning hours. While the early risers begin to stream through the front doors, our bakers pull tray after tray of pastries from the ovens, filling the air with seductive aromas of butter and cinnamon. Breakfast seems to evoke the most powerful food memories. Perhaps because it recalls earlier times when the simple pleasure of homemade breakfasts was a way of life, or maybe because it serves as a delicious harbinger for the day to come. Whatever the reason, many folks treasure their morning routine of a hot cup of coffee and a buttery, flaky croissant at their neighborhood bakery.

We had hoped that as a neighborhood bakery we would become a staple in the social life of the community. Over the last eighteen years, we've found that nothing is more gratifying than being part of the early morning rituals of our customers.

Our aim as bakers is to create comforting and delicious food from the freshest ingredients available. We really don't care for sugary baked goods, and our customers often tell us they appreciate that our pastries aren't overly sweet. Our breakfast pastry repertoire is small, yet each recipe lends itself to nearly unlimited variations allowing us to indulge our craving for variety. We hope you'll use these recipes as a point of departure for your own favorite fillings or additions.

Professional and home bakers alike love baking powder and soda-leavened pastries with good reason—they're fast and easy to make. For example, you can enjoy scones hot from the oven for breakfast by measuring the wet and dry ingredients a day or two before, then simply mixing and baking in the morning.

If you're new to baking with yeast you may think it's complicated but we've tried to guide you through the process by sharing the tips and tricks that work for us every day in the bakery.

BUTTER CROISSANTS

When you bite into a perfect croissant the delicate exterior will shatter into a cascade of tiny flakes of pastry. The open honeycombed interior is formed of paper thin leaves of dough so moist they fuse together when pressed. It's possible to make this recipe at home over a weekend if you wish to serve warm croissants on Sunday morning, or you can freeze the dough to shape and bake at a future date. See tips on working with the dough on page 27. *MAKES 12 CROISSANTS*

630 GRAMS (4½ CUPS) ALL-PURPOSE FLOUR

7 GRAMS (2¼ TEASPOONS) INSTANT YEAST

50 GRAMS (¼ CUP) SUGAR

14 GRAMS (2½ TEASPOONS) SALT

28 GRAMS (2 TABLESPOONS) UNSALTED BUTTER, COOL ROOM TEMPERATURE, CUBED

186 GRAMS (¾ CUP) WATER, ROOM TEMPERATURE (ABOUT 70 DEGREES)

186 GRAMS (¾ CUP) MILK, ROOM TEMPERATURE (ABOUT 70 DEGREES)

Butter for roll-in:
280 GRAMS (10 OUNCES) UNSALTED BUTTER, CHILLED

Egg wash:
1 EGG
PINCH SALT

Mixing the dough:

Total active time: about 20 minutes. Inactive time: 6 to 8 hours if shaping on the same day, or 1 hour plus an overnight rest if shaping the next day.

1. In a large bowl, whisk together the flour, yeast, sugar, and salt. Using your fingertips, rub the butter into the dry ingredients until it's evenly distributed and coated with the dry ingredients.

2. In the bowl of a stand mixer fitted with the dough hook, combine the water and milk. Add the dry ingredients on low speed and incorporate for 3 minutes, stopping once to scrape down the sides of the bowl. Increase to medium speed, stopping the mixer after 2 minutes to check the consistency of the dough. The dough should be a medium-soft consistency. If the dough feels stiff, add more water a tablespoon at a time. (Note: if it climbs the sides of the bowl during the mixing, stop the mixer and push it back down around the hook, as many times as needed.)

3. Continue mixing on medium speed for a total of about 4 minutes. The surface won't be completely smooth, but the dough will hold together. You could also mix the dough in a food processor, pulsing for about 2 minutes or until the dough forms a ball. It's important not to over mix, as the dough will become more difficult to roll out and result in a less tender croissant.

4. Cover the bowl loosely with plastic wrap and set it aside to rise in a warm room (75 degrees is ideal for both dough and room) for about 1 hour, or until it's increased in volume by about half.

5. Transfer the dough to a lightly floured work surface and press it into a rectangle about 2 inches thick. Wrap it in plastic wrap (seal it well as the dough will be rising and may seep out of any openings) and refrigerate for a minimum of 4 hours or overnight.

Preparing the butter for roll-in:

Total active time: about 5 minutes. Inactive time: about 20 minutes.

1. About 30 minutes before rolling out the dough, chop the chilled butter into large chunks and place it in the bowl of a stand mixer fitted with the dough hook. On medium speed, beat the butter until completely smooth and pliable but not warm, about 3 minutes.

2. Scrape the butter out of the bowl onto a piece of plastic wrap or parchment paper. Press it into a 6-inch square about ½ inch thick. Chill it in the refrigerator for about 15 minutes or until it's just firm, not hard.

3. Alternatively, to prepare the butter by hand, place it on a piece of parchment paper or plastic wrap on a countertop. Using a French rolling pin pound the butter until it's flat and pliable. Follow the directions above for shaping and chilling.

Rolling out (laminating) the dough:

Total time: 2 to 2½ hours plus a final 2-hour rest before shaping, unless you freeze the dough for shaping at a future date.

1. The room temperature and work surface of your work area should be on the cool side, and each step should be done as quickly as possible to prevent the dough from warming up and the butter from softening. Gather all of your tools and flour for dusting and place them within hands' reach.

2. If the butter feels firm, remove it from the refrigerator a few minutes before you're ready to begin laminating the dough. Otherwise, dust the work surface lightly with flour, then remove the dough and the butter block from the refrigerator, unwrap the dough and place it on the floured surface. Roll the dough into a rectangle that is twice the size of your butter square, 12 inches long by 6 inches wide. Brush the surface of the dough to remove any loose flour, unwrap the butter square and place it on one half of the rectangle. The edges of the butter and the dough should be neatly stacked. Fold the other half of the rectangle over the butter and press or pinch the three open sides together to seal the butter in the dough.

3. Flour the work surface lightly again, if needed, and roll out the dough into a rectangle about ½ inch thick, about twice as long as it is wide, with a long side of the rectangle facing you. Brush the surface of the dough to remove any loose flour. Fold the dough lengthwise in thirds, as if folding a business letter. First fold the left third over the center of the rectangle. Brush off any loose flour from the surface of the dough and fold the right third over the left. Straighten and

square the edges so that the layers are neatly stacked using the side of your hand or a bench knife. This is the first turn, also called a single or envelope fold. Wrap the dough in plastic wrap and refrigerate it for 45 minutes to 1 hour to relax the gluten.

4. For the second turn, scrape the work surface free of any dough particles and dust it lightly with flour. Remove the dough from the refrigerator, unwrap it, and place it on the work surface with the long folded side facing you. Roll the dough out as before into a ½-inch-thick rectangle. Fold the dough into thirds, brushing off the excess flour between folds. Wrap and refrigerate the dough for 45 minutes to 1 hour.

5. For the third and final turn, repeat the folding steps above. Wrap and refrigerate the dough for at least 2 hours before the final shaping. If you plan to shape the croissants the following morning, place the dough in the freezer and transfer it to the refrigerator before going to bed. The dough may be frozen for up to 10 days after the final turn, then thawed in the refrigerator overnight before shaping.

Final shaping and proofing:

Total active time: 30 minutes. Inactive time: 1½ to 2 hours proofing time.

1. Line 2 half-size (13 by 18-inch) baking sheets with parchment paper and set them aside.

2. On a lightly floured work surface, roll the dough into a 12-inch-wide by 25-inch-long rectangle, ¼ inch thick. Lightly dust the dough and the work surface with flour as needed to prevent sticking. If the dough springs back and is difficult to lengthen, allow it to rest a few minutes before continuing. When the desired length is reached, use a pizza wheel or chef's knife to trim and straighten the narrow ends. Cut the rectangle into long, skinny triangles, 4 inches wide at their base and 10 to 12 inches long on the sides. Make a ¾-inch-long incision in the center of each 4-inch base (this helps to create the desired length in the final shape).

3. To shape each croissant, pick up the triangle, holding the base with one hand. With the other hand about 1 inch from the base, pull on the dough gently to lengthen it slightly, being careful not to cause tears on the surface. Place the triangle back down on the work surface with the base towards you and gently but firmly roll it away from you towards the tip. The small cut made in the base helps in lengthening the croissant. If done properly, you should have 6 to 7 tiers. As you shape each croissant, place it on the lined baking sheet, evenly spaced, making sure that the tip of each croissant sits firmly underneath the rolled dough.

4. When all the croissants are placed on the baking sheets, prepare the egg wash. Whisk the egg, 2 teaspoons of water, and salt together in a small bowl until smooth. Using a pastry brush, brush each croissant lightly with the egg wash, carefully avoiding the open edges as the egg may "glue" them together and prevent the tiers from rising fully. Cover and refrigerate the egg wash to use later on for the final egg washing.

5. Set the baking sheets aside in a relatively warm (75 to 78 degrees), draft-free space and let the croissants rise 1½ to 2 hours. A good spot would be in an unheated oven with a pan of hot, steaming water placed on the bottom to provide humidity, which helps prevent a skin from forming on the shaped croissants. It's important to keep the croissants cool enough to prevent the butter layers from melting, which would make them greasy and affect the flakiness.

6. About half an hour before baking, remove the proofing croissants from the oven, if using. Position the oven racks in the upper and lower thirds of the oven and preheat to 430 degrees. The croissants will be ready to go in the oven when they have almost doubled in volume and the dough springs back slightly when pressed gently with a fingertip. Each tier will still hold a distinct shape. (Note: Since room conditions, humidity, and flour quality all affect the proofing time, it's impossible to give a precise time that would work in all situations. Check the croissants frequently after the first hour. If the dough over proofs, the croissants will have a bread-like texture. If the room temperature is too warm, the butter will melt, yielding dense, greasy pastries.)

7. A few minutes before you are ready to bake the croissants, brush them with another thin coat of egg wash, again carefully avoiding the edges of the tiers. Bake for 10 minutes then quickly open the oven door and rotate the baking sheets from top to bottom and front to back for even coloring. Continue baking for another 4 to 6 minutes until the croissants are evenly baked, with deeply browned, crisp edges. Remove from the oven and transfer the croissants to a wire rack to cool slightly. They are best when eaten while still warm or just shortly after baking.

Working with Croissant Dough

The croissant achieves its light delicate texture from a process called lamination. The dough is wrapped around a block of butter, then rolled out and folded several times, creating scores of light buttery layers. If it's your first time making croissants it may be challenging, but it shouldn't be difficult. If your dough feels elastic and resists rolling out, allow it to rest for a few minutes before continuing. The main key to success is keeping your butter and dough chilled as you work. If the butter softens during lamination, place the dough back in the refrigerator briefly until the butter is firm. Then continue the rolling and folding process.

In the bakery our timing is precise by necessity, but at home you have the luxury of working in a more leisurely fashion, keeping in mind the following tips:

Plan ahead: Read through the entire recipe carefully before starting. There are several resting steps built in to the process that you don't want to rush. And since you may want to hold your dough overnight or maybe 2 nights, this will help you to create a timetable that fits conveniently into your schedule.

Preparation: Find a cool room temperature area to work in, if possible. Have all your tools near at hand before starting, including a small bowl of flour for dusting the work surface, a rolling pin, and a pastry brush. A bench knife is helpful, too.

Butter temperature and texture: The butter for roll-in should be pliable, but not too firm or soft. Its texture and temperature should be similar to your dough. Butter that contains a high butter fat content will give you better and more consistent results (see page 18), but isn't essential.

A note about measuring ingredients: We've given weight measurements in this recipe because it is a much more accurate way of measuring, especially for dry ingredients. In the bakery, we use only weight measurements—not only is it more precise, it's helpful when buying ingredients that are sold or packaged by weight, like nuts, chocolate, and fruit. Using a scale helps to eliminate errors when increasing or decreasing recipes and allows you to become familiar with the proportion of ingredients, which gives you a better understanding of why a recipe works. For the home baker, a good kitchen scale is a small investment that will quickly become your most reliable tool.

PAIN AU CHOCOLAT

Roll out the dough as described in Step 2. Square the edges by trimming them with a sharp knife or pizza cutter. Cut the dough in half lengthwise, then cut it into 6 x 4-inch rectangles, with the narrower edges facing you. Along the far edge of each rectangle, lightly brush a strip of egg wash. Place two bittersweet chocolate batons (see Sources page 175), or about 1 ounce of chocolate chunks, on the near edge of each rectangle. Begin rolling the dough by enclosing the chocolate. Finish the rolling by centering the seam underneath and pressing down lightly to help seal the dough. Follow the proofing and baking instructions for Butter Croissants. *MAKES 12 PAIN AU CHOCOLAT*

HAM AND CHEESE CROISSANT

After cutting the croissant dough into triangles, place 1 ounce of thinly sliced ham, 1 tablespoon of a grated, hard, aged cheese like Parmigiano-Reggiano or Asiago, and some freshly ground black pepper to taste on the wider end leaving about 2 inches from the narrow tip uncovered. Follow the shaping, proofing, and baking as for Butter Croissants.

ALMOND CROISSANT

This is a great way to use croissants that are day-old or frozen. If frozen, thaw at room temperature for a couple of hours or the night before you plan to make these. *MAKES 6 ALMOND CROISSANTS*

6 BUTTER CROISSANTS, BAKED AND COOLED
1 RECIPE SUGAR SYRUP
1 RECIPE FRANGIPANE (PAGE 168)
SLICED ALMONDS, FOR GARNISH
CONFECTIONERS' SUGAR FOR DUSTING

Sugar Syrup:
½ CUP SUGAR
DROP OF ALMOND EXTRACT

1. To make the Sugar Syrup, in a small saucepan bring the sugar and ½ cup of water to a boil. Remove from the heat and add the drop of extract. Cool before using.

2. Slice each croissant horizontally. Brush the cut sides of each half with sugar syrup. Spread the bottom halves with about 2 tablespoons of frangipane, replace the top halves, and smear about 1 tablespoon of frangipane across each top. Sprinkle a few sliced almonds on top and arrange on a parchment-lined baking sheet. Bake in a preheated 350 degree oven for about 15 minutes or until the frangipane on top is firm and the croissant is heated throughout and crispy. Remove from the oven and transfer to a wire rack to cool slightly. Dust with confectioners' sugar.

MORNING BUNS

At once crispy and moist, with a slight hint of cinnamon, these buttery rolls remind my husband of french toast. The variation on the following page, rolled in cinnamon sugar, is the version I tried the very first time I tasted one of these habit-forming pastries at a bakery near San Francisco. If you loved cinnamon toast as a kid, these are the ones you should try. Sprinkle some coarsely chopped walnuts into each muffin tin if desired. A.P. *MAKES 12 BUNS*

1½ CUPS PACKED DARK BROWN SUGAR
1¼ TEASPOON GROUND CINNAMON
1 RECIPE CROISSANT DOUGH, RESTED AND CHILLED (PAGE 23)

1. In a small bowl, combine the brown sugar and cinnamon.

2. Butter a 12-cup muffin pan, including the top surface, and place a firmly packed teaspoon of the brown sugar mixture in each of the cups. Spread it loosely over the bottom of the cup.

3. On a lightly floured surface, roll out the croissant dough into a rectangle about 9 inches wide, 22 inches long, and ¼ inch thick, with a long side facing you. Spread 1 cup of the brown sugar mixture evenly over the top. Beginning with the side closest to you, roll the dough firmly into a log. Place the seam edge on the bottom and brush off any loose flour from the surface.

4. With a sharp knife, slice the log into 1¾-inch-thick slices. Place the slices into the prepared muffin pan, cut side down.

5. Set the muffin tin aside to rise in a moderately warm, draft-proof area to proof for 1½ to 2 hours, depending on the temperature of the room and dough. When ready, the buns will be about double in size and will spring back slowly when pressed with your fingertip.

6. Position a rack in the center of the oven and preheat the oven to 375 degrees.

7. Place the muffin tin on a baking sheet and bake for 30 to 35 minutes, rotating the sheet after the first 15 minutes. When done, the pastries will be medium brown and firm to the touch. To check for doneness, carefully pull two buns apart. If there is any translucency, continue baking until opaque.

8. Line a baking sheet with parchment paper. Remove the pan from the oven, and being extremely careful to avoid burning yourself, flip the muffin tin away from you onto the prepared baking sheet. It may need a gentle shake to release every piece. Carefully scrape out any sugar syrup stuck in the tin with a wooden spoon and drizzle it over the pastries.

9. Let cool for a few minutes and serve warm.

CINNAMON BUN

3½ CUPS SUGAR

2 TABLESPOONS PLUS 1 TEASPOON GROUND CINNAMON

1 RECIPE CROISSANT DOUGH, RESTED AND CHILLED (PAGE 23)

1. Combine the sugar and the cinnamon in a medium bowl. Set 1 cup of the cinnamon sugar aside for the filling. Butter a 12-cup muffin pan. Follow the recipe for Morning Buns from Step 3, substituting 1 cup of cinnamon sugar for the brown sugar mixture. Allow the buns to cool for about 10 minutes. Toss the warm buns one by one in the cinnamon sugar until they have a light, even coating. Serve immediately.

CURRANT SCONES

The quintessential scone—firm yet tender, hand cut, and speckled with moist currants. Instead of cream, which is more commonly used, these contain yogurt to balance the sweetness and brown sugar, which gives a deeper complexity to the flavor. Clear Flour Bread in Brookline, Massachusetts, has made this scone for almost thirty years. It's been on our menu since we opened seventeen years ago, and we've baked some version of it every day since then.

Note: For the lightest, flakiest scones be sure to keep your butter and yogurt chilled until you are ready to add them to the dough. The scones will have more of a cake-like texture if the butter is reduced too far, so pea-size butter chunks are essential. Lastly, tossing the wet and dry ingredients with a plastic scraper and then using your hands until the mass just holds together will prevent excessive development of gluten in the flour, and give you a fine, tender crumb. *MAKES 12 SCONES*

¾ CUP DRIED CURRANTS

4 CUPS ALL-PURPOSE FLOUR

⅓ CUP PLUS 1 TABLESPOON PACKED DARK BROWN SUGAR

1 TABLESPOON BAKING POWDER

1 TEASPOON BAKING SODA

1½ TEASPOONS SALT

⅔ CUP (1¼ STICK) UNSALTED BUTTER, CUT INTO ½-INCH CUBES, CHILLED

1½ CUPS NON-FAT PLAIN YOGURT

For the garnish:

¼ CUP SUGAR

1½ TEASPOONS GROUND CINNAMON

1. In a small bowl, cover the currants with hot water and soak for 5 minutes. Drain and set aside.

2. Make the cinnamon sugar garnish. In a small bowl, combine sugar and cinnamon and set aside.

3. Position a rack in the middle of the oven and preheat the oven to 425 degrees. Line a baking sheet with parchment paper.

4. In a large bowl, whisk together the flour, brown sugar, baking powder, baking soda, and salt. Break up any remaining lumps with your fingertips.

5. Add the cubed butter and work it into the flour mixture with your fingertips until a few pea-size chunks of butter remain.

6. Add the currants and toss until they're evenly distributed. Add the yogurt and, using your hands or a plastic scraper, combine just until the dough holds together. Be careful not to over mix or the tenderness of the scone will be affected.

7. Transfer the dough to a lightly floured work surface or silicone mat. Gently form it into an 8-inch square, 1¼ inches thick. Sprinkle the cinnamon sugar over the top. Using a sharp knife or bench knife, cut the dough into six squares. Cut each square in half on the diagonal.

8. Transfer each triangle to the baking sheet, placing the scones about 1½ inches apart.

9. Bake for 15 to 18 minutes, rotating the baking sheet after 10 minutes for even baking. The scones will be golden brown on the edges and feel firm in the center.

10. Remove from the oven and transfer the scones to a wire rack to cool slightly before serving.

Variations:

CRANBERRY WALNUT SCONES

Substitute ¾ cup dried, sweetened cranberries and ⅓ cup chopped walnuts for the currants. Instead of cinnamon sugar, dust with turbinado sugar.

APRICOT ALMOND SCONES

Substitute ¾ cup dried, chopped apricots and ⅓ cup toasted, chopped almonds (see instructions on page 170) for the currants. Instead of cinnamon sugar, dust with turbinado sugar.

WILD BLUEBERRY OAT SCONES

A moist cream scone brimming with fresh fruit, that is both melt-in-your-mouth tender and nourishing. Simple to make and quick to put together, it's perfect for a summer day when you have baskets of freshly picked berries on hand. Since wild blueberries don't lose their zest when frozen, we often extend the season and bake these into the cooler months—a treat when the season has passed and we're missing the bounty of summer fruit. Oats being cultivated in the same regions as blueberries, the flavors pair harmoniously while also adding a textural contrast to the moist fruit.

Note: The most you can fit on a baking sheet is 6. If you have only one baking sheet, position the rack in the center of the oven. The additional dough can sit at cool room temperature while the first batch is baking. After the baking sheet has cooled, you can bake the last round. Note that the second batch may be taller and rounder than the first because the oats have a tendency to absorb moisture as the mixture sits. *MAKES 9 SCONES*

2½ CUPS ALL-PURPOSE FLOUR

¼ CUP PACKED DARK BROWN SUGAR

1 TABLESPOON PLUS ¼ TEASPOON BAKING POWDER

¾ TEASPOON BAKING SODA

¾ TEASPOON SALT

9 TABLESPOONS (1 STICK PLUS 1 TABLESPOON) UNSALTED
  BUTTER, CUT INTO ½-INCH CUBES, CHILLED

¾ CUP ROLLED OATS, PLUS MORE FOR GARNISH

¾ CUP FRESH OR FROZEN WILD BLUEBERRIES

1½ CUPS HALF-AND-HALF

1 TEASPOON VANILLA EXTRACT

2 TABLESPOONS TURBINADO SUGAR, FOR GARNISH

1. Position racks in the upper and lower thirds of the oven and preheat the oven to 350 degrees. Line two baking sheets with parchment paper.

2. In a large bowl, whisk together the flour, brown sugar, baking powder, baking soda, and salt. Break up any remaining lumps with your fingertips.

3. Add the cubed butter and using your fingertips work it into the flour mixture until a few pea-size chunks of butter remain. Add the oats and the blueberries and toss everything together using your hands, until the blueberries are coated with the dry ingredients.

4. In a glass measuring cup with a spout, combine the half-and-half and vanilla. Gradually add the liquid to the flour mixture, using a rubber spatula or plastic scraper. Mix until the dough just comes together (the dough will be very moist).

5. Using a ½-cup measuring cup for each scone, loosely scoop the dough and drop it in mounds onto the prepared baking sheet, spacing them about 3 inches apart. Garnish the tops with the additional oats, then dust them with the turbinado sugar.

6. Bake for 25 to 27 minutes, rotating the baking sheet after 15 minutes for even baking. They will have golden brown ridges and feel firm in the center.

7. Remove from the oven and transfer the scones to a wire rack to cool slightly before serving.

A moist cream scone brimming with fresh fruit, that is both melt-in-your-mouth tender and nourishing. It's perfect for a summer day.

PUMPKIN CREAM SCONES

Just as the leaves turn to gold and crimson, the smell of warm pumpkin scones is the bakery's own sign of autumn's approach. These seasonal scones are so comforting on a chilly fall morning, with just the right amount of warm spices and pieces of ginger. *MAKES 12 SCONES*

2½ CUPS ALL-PURPOSE FLOUR

¼ CUP PACKED DARK BROWN SUGAR

1 TABLESPOON PLUS ½ TEASPOON BAKING POWDER

½ TEASPOON SALT

1¾ TEASPOONS GROUND CINNAMON

1¼ TEASPOONS GROUND GINGER

1¼ TEASPOONS GROUND NUTMEG

1 TEASPOON GROUND ALLSPICE

½ CUP PLUS 2 TABLESPOONS (1¼ STICKS) UNSALTED
   BUTTER, CUT INTO ½-INCH CUBES, CHILLED

⅓ CUP FINELY DICED CRYSTALLIZED GINGER

1 EGG

¾ CUP PUMPKIN PUREE

⅓ CUP HALF-AND-HALF

2 TABLESPOONS MOLASSES

For the garnish:

⅓ CUP GRANULATED SUGAR

⅛ TEASPOON GROUND CINNAMON

⅓ CUP PUMPKIN SEEDS

1. Position a rack in the center of the oven and preheat the oven to 400 degrees. Line a baking sheet with parchment paper.

2. Make the cinnamon sugar garnish. In a small bowl, combine sugar and cinnamon and set aside.

3. In a large bowl, whisk together the flour, brown sugar, baking powder, salt, cinnamon, ground ginger, nutmeg, and allspice. Break up any remaining lumps with your fingertips.

4. Add the cubed butter and using your fingertips work it into the flour mixture until a few pea-size chunks of butter remain. Add the crystallized ginger and toss until it's evenly distributed.

5. In a separate bowl, whisk together the egg, pumpkin puree, half-and-half, and molasses. Pour

this mixture into the dry ingredients and, using your hands or a rubber spatula, fold everything together until the dry ingredients are evenly moistened. It's important not to over mix at this stage or the scones will be tough.

6. With an ice cream scoop, drop golf ball-size mounds onto the baking sheet, about 2½ inches apart.

7. Top each scone with a few pumpkin seeds and dust with cinnamon sugar. Bake for 23 to 25 minutes, rotating the baking sheet after 12 minutes for even baking. They will be golden brown and feel firm in the center.

8. Remove from the oven and transfer the scones to a wire rack to cool slightly before serving.

PEAR GINGER SCONES

We make these scones for a few weeks after the holidays every year. Initially, we created them to utilize the dried pears we had left over from our Christmas Stollen. Now we order extra fruit so that we can bake these gorgeous scones. The process of drying pears concentrates their sweet, subtle flavor. These cinnamon-and-ginger-spiced scones have pockets of these intense gems throughout. Dried pears can be a bit difficult to find at your local grocery, but are worth seeking out from a specialty food store. *MAKES 12 SCONES*

¾ CUP DRIED PEARS, CHOPPED

1 CUP WATER, BOILING

1 EGG PLUS 1 YOLK

⅔ CUP HALF-AND-HALF

1 TEASPOON VANILLA EXTRACT

2¾ CUPS ALL-PURPOSE FLOUR

¼ CUP PACKED DARK BROWN SUGAR

1 TABLESPOON PLUS ½ TEASPOON BAKING POWDER

1 TEASPOON SALT

½ TEASPOON GROUND CINNAMON

½ CUP (1 STICK) UNSALTED BUTTER, CUT INTO ½-INCH CUBES, CHILLED

¼ CUP CHOPPED CRYSTALLIZED GINGER

For the garnish:

¼ CUP SUGAR

1½ TEASPOONS GROUND CINNAMON

1. Position a rack in the center of the oven and preheat the oven to 375 degrees. Line a baking sheet with parchment paper.

2. Place the dried pears in a heatproof bowl and pour the boiling water over them. Let them sit for 15 minutes to rehydrate. Drain the pears well and set them aside to cool.

3. Make the cinnamon sugar garnish. In a small bowl, combine the sugar and cinnamon and set aside.

4. In a small bowl, whisk together the egg, yolk, half-and-half, and vanilla.

5. In a large bowl, whisk together the flour, brown sugar, baking powder, salt, and cinnamon. Break up any remaining lumps with your fingertips.

6. Add the cubed butter to the flour mixture and using your fingertips work it in until a few pea-size chunks of butter remain.

7. Add the egg mixture to the dry ingredients and combine them using a fork or your hands until the dry ingredients are fully moistened.

8. Fold in the drained pears and the ginger until they are evenly distributed.

9. Using an ice cream scoop or a ¼ cup measuring cup gently fill the scoop and drop evenly spaced mounds onto the baking sheet.

10. Sprinkle lightly with cinnamon sugar.

11. Bake for 23 to 25 minutes, rotating the baking sheet after 12 minutes for even baking. They will be golden and feel firm in the center.

12. Remove from the oven and transfer the scones to a wire rack to cool slightly before serving.

CHEDDAR CHIVE SCONES

When the aromas of sweet golden cornmeal, tangy buttery cheese, and fragrant chives are emanating from the oven, a craving for a savory breakfast overcomes us. This tender, wholesome biscuit is exactly what we reach for when we don't want a sweet pastry or snack. It is also the perfect accompaniment to a bowl of soup or chili. The cornmeal and cheese topping creates a crunchy crust to contrast the tender crumb inside. *MAKES 12 SCONES*

For the scones:
2 CUPS ALL-PURPOSE FLOUR
⅓ CUP STONE-GROUND CORNMEAL
2 TABLESPOONS SUGAR

1 TABLESPOON BAKING POWDER

1 TEASPOON SALT

2 TEASPOONS COARSELY GROUND BLACK PEPPER

½ CUP (1 STICK) UNSALTED BUTTER,
   CUT INTO ½-INCH CUBES, CHILLED

1 EGG

¾ CUP HALF-AND-HALF

¼ CUP FINELY CHOPPED FRESH CHIVES

1½ CUPS (ABOUT 6 OUNCES) GRATED
   SHARP CHEDDAR CHEESE

For the topping:

¼ CUP STONE-GROUND CORNMEAL

½ CUP GRATED SHARP CHEDDAR CHEESE

½ TEASPOON COARSELY GROUND BLACK PEPPER

1. Position a rack in the center of the oven and preheat the oven to 400 degrees. Line a baking sheet with parchment paper.

2. Make the topping by combining the cornmeal, cheese, and pepper in a food processor fitted with the blade attachment. Pulse on and off until the texture resembles a course meal. Transfer to a small bowl and set aside.

3. In a large bowl, whisk together the flour, cornmeal, sugar, baking powder, salt, and pepper. Break up any remaining lumps with your fingertips.

4. Add the cubed butter and work it into the flour mixture using your fingertips until a few pea-size chunks of butter remain.

5. In a small bowl, whisk together the egg and half-and-half. Pour into the flour mixture and, using your hands or a rubber spatula, fold everything together until the dry ingredients are evenly moistened.

6. Add the chives and cheese and mix until just combined.

7. With an ice cream scoop, scoop a golf ball-size portion and dip it into the topping mixture to coat. Place it onto the prepared baking sheet with the topping facing up. Repeat with the rest of the dough, evenly spacing the mounds on the baking sheet, about 2 inches apart.

8. Bake for 23 to 25 minutes, rotating the baking sheet after 12 minutes for even baking. They will be golden brown and feel firm in the center.

9. Remove from the oven and transfer the scones to a wire rack to cool slightly before serving.

CHOCOLATE BABKA

The babka has its origins in Eastern Europe and it is steeped in Polish and Jewish tradition. A yeast-risen cake that traditionally contained fruit filling, raisins, and an icing, today there are countless versions and variations. There are as many ways to shape a babka as there are delicious fillings to fold inside. Our interpretation is a rich, coffee-cake style, with swirls of filling and crumbly streusel. Chocolate is always a favorite flavor, but the hazelnut and apricot cream cheese adaptations have very loyal fans as well.

Note: We use Boyajian lemon oil in the bakery. It can be purchased online through King Arthur Flour and other specialty food stores listed in the Sources (page 175). Chocolate Walnut Biscotti (pages 122-124) or Chocolate Sablé (pages 132-133) are great choices for this recipe. Pulse in a food processor until fine crumbs remain. *MAKES ONE 9-INCH LOAF*

For the dough:
1¾ CUPS PLUS 2 TABLESPOONS BREAD FLOUR
2 TABLESPOONS PLUS 1 TEASPOON SUGAR
½ TEASPOON SALT
1 TEASPOON INSTANT YEAST
1 EGG, ROOM TEMPERATURE
⅓ CUP WHOLE MILK, ROOM TEMPERATURE
⅛ TEASPOON ALMOND EXTRACT
2 DROPS LEMON OIL
1 TABLESPOON PLUS 1 TEASPOON
  UNSALTED BUTTER, SOFTENED

For the chocolate filling:
⅓ CUP (¾ STICK) UNSALTED BUTTER
⅓ CUP PACKED LIGHT BROWN SUGAR
2 TABLESPOONS ALL-PURPOSE FLOUR
2 TABLESPOONS DUTCH-PROCESSED
  COCOA POWDER
PINCH SALT
1 TABLESPOON HONEY
1 EGG
¼ TEASPOON VANILLA EXTRACT
⅓ CUP CHOCOLATE COOKIE CRUMBS

For the egg wash:
1 EGG
PINCH SALT
½ CUP STREUSEL (PAGE 170)

1. To make the dough, combine the flour, sugar, salt, and yeast in the bowl of a stand mixer fitted with the dough hook and stir to combine.

2. In a small bowl, whisk together the egg, milk, almond extract, and lemon oil.

3. Add the egg mixture and the softened butter to the dry ingredients and mix on medium low speed for 4 minutes, until a smooth dough is formed. Roll the dough into a ball and place it in a bowl. Cover the bowl with plastic wrap, place in a warm area (75 to 80 degrees) and let the dough rest for 1 hour.

4. While the dough is resting, you can make the filling. In a small saucepan, melt the butter over low heat. Remove from the heat to cool. In a medium bowl, stir together the brown sugar, flour, cocoa, and salt. In a small bowl, mix together the cooled melted butter, honey, egg, and vanilla. Add the egg mixture to the dry ingredients and beat until smooth. Stir in the cookie crumbs and set aside.

5. Lightly grease a 9-inch loaf pan with nonstick cooking spray.

6. To shape the babka, flour a work surface lightly and roll out the dough to a rectangle, 10 inches by 24 inches, with the long edge facing you. Lightly dust the top of the dough and the work surface with flour as needed to prevent the dough from sticking to the table or the rolling pin. If the dough shrinks back as you are rolling it out, cover it loosely with plastic wrap and let it rest a few minutes. Continue this process until you have reached the right dimensions.

7. Brush any loose flour from the surface of the dough, then spread the filling over the top, leaving a half-inch border along the top and bottom edges.

8. Starting with the bottom edge, roll the dough into the middle of the rectangle and do the same with the top edge so that the two rolls meet in the center.

9. Visualize the rolls divided into three equal lengths. Fold the left third over onto the middle third. Then fold the right third over the middle third.

10. Pick up the dough and turn it over so that the seam end is on the bottom. Then, holding each end, give it a single gentle twist in the middle and place it in the prepared pan.

11. To make the egg wash, whisk together the egg, 1 teaspoon of water, and salt in a small bowl.

12. Using a pastry brush, coat the top of the babka lightly with egg wash, and cover the pan with plastic wrap. Save the remaining egg wash in the refrigerator for later. Place the babka in a warm, draft-free area to rise for 1½ to 2 hours. It is ready when the dough holds a dimple when pressed lightly with a finger.

13. Position a rack in the center of the oven and preheat the oven to 375 degrees.

14. Brush the babka with egg wash again and spread the streusel evenly over the top.

15. Bake for 50 minutes, rotating the pan from front to back half way through the baking time. The babka should be a deep golden brown and a probe thermometer should read 190 degrees when inserted into the center of the loaf. Remove from the oven and allow it to cool in the pan for 15 minutes before turning it out onto a wire rack. Serve warm or at room temperature. It can be wrapped with plastic wrap and stored for 1 to 2 days at room temperature.

HAZELNUT BABKA

Substitute this cinnamon-laced nut filling for the chocolate filling. You could also try other nuts, such as almonds or walnuts.

⅓ CUP SUGAR

¼ CUP MILK

3 TABLESPOONS UNSALTED BUTTER

¼ TEASPOON VANILLA EXTRACT

PINCH SALT

1¼ CUPS HAZELNUTS, TOASTED, SKINNED, AND FINELY CHOPPED (SEE INSTRUCTIONS ON PAGE 170)

⅛ TEASPOON GROUND CINNAMON

1 EGG YOLK

1. In a medium saucepan, combine the sugar, milk, butter, vanilla, and salt. Heat just until the mixture comes to a boil.

2. Remove the pot from the heat and add the hazelnuts and cinnamon. Stir until combined, then transfer the mixture to a bowl to cool.

3. When the mixture is completely cool, whisk in the egg yolk.

4. Follow instructions above for shaping and baking.

APRICOT CREAM CHEESE BABKA

This apricot filling has just the right amount of sweet and tart notes. We found a winning combination when we blended it with smooth cream cheese and buttery pastry.

1 RECIPE CREAM CHEESE FILLING (PAGE 167)
½ CUP ORANGE JUICE
⅓ CUP LEMON JUICE
1½ CUPS DRIED APRICOTS
⅛ CUP SUGAR

1. Combine the orange juice, lemon juice, apricots, and sugar in a medium saucepan. Simmer over medium-low heat for about 20 minutes, until the dried fruit softens and the liquid is reduced by about half. Remove it from the heat and let it cool.

2. Place the cooled mixture in a food processor fitted with the blade attachment and process until a smooth jam is formed.

3. Smooth the apricot filling over the top of the rolled-out dough, leaving a ½-inch border along the top and bottom edges. Spread the cream cheese filling over the apricot layer.

4. Follow instructions above for shaping and baking.

FRENCH PUFFS

The hint of fresh nutmeg, tangy buttermilk, and dusting of cinnamon sugar may conjure up cake doughnut daydreams, but baked in this diminutive shape, this little cake is at home on the fanciest of brunch tables. To get a nice, even coating of cinnamon sugar, it's best to allow a few minutes for the puff to absorb the melted butter. *MAKES 24 PUFFS*

2⅔ CUPS ALL-PURPOSE FLOUR

¾ TEASPOON SALT

1½ TEASPOONS BAKING POWDER

¼ TEASPOON BAKING SODA

1 TEASPOON FRESHLY GRATED NUTMEG

¾ CUP (1½ STICKS) UNSALTED BUTTER,
  ROOM TEMPERATURE, PLUS MORE FOR GREASING PAN

⅓ CUP GRANULATED SUGAR

⅓ CUP PACKED DARK BROWN SUGAR

2 EGGS, ROOM TEMPERATURE

1 TEASPOON VANILLA EXTRACT

1 CUP BUTTERMILK, ROOM TEMPERATURE

For the topping:

4 TABLESPOONS BUTTER, MELTED

¼ TEASPOON VANILLA EXTRACT

¼ CUP SUGAR

1½ TEASPOONS GROUND CINNAMON

1. Position a rack in the center of the oven and preheat to 425 degrees. Lightly butter a 24-cup mini-muffin tin.

2. In a large bowl, whisk together the flour, salt, baking powder, baking soda, and nutmeg.

3. In the bowl of a stand mixer fitted with the paddle attachment, cream together the butter and sugars on medium speed until smooth. Reduce to low speed and beat in the eggs one at a time. Add the vanilla and half the buttermilk, beating to combine well after each addition. Stop the mixer occasionally to scrape down the sides of the bowl and paddle using a plastic scraper or rubber spatula.

4. On low speed slowly add half the dry ingredients and beat until just incorporated.

5. Add the remaining buttermilk followed by the rest of the dry ingredients. Mix until the batter is smooth and all the ingredients are fully combined.

6. Scoop the batter into the prepared muffin tins, about two heaping tablespoons per cup. The batter will mound up over the top of the cups. Bake for 14 minutes, rotating the tray half way through the baking time. The cakes will feel firm when pressed gently on the tops.

7. Remove from the oven and place on a cooling rack to cool for a few minutes. While the puffs are still warm, add the vanilla to the melted butter, dip the tops of each puff and set aside. In a small bowl, combine the sugar and cinnamon, then roll each puff in the cinnamon sugar until it's coated with a thin, uniform layer. These are heavenly when served still warm from the oven.

EARLY MORNINGS

Every morning from January through December our bakers begin their days work at 3 A.M. The front door is unlocked, the lights go on, the ovens are fired up, and work garb and aprons are donned. The sweet bread doughs and Viennoiserie are pulled from the walk-in refrigerators for their final rise or "proof" before going into the ovens. For the bakers, all musings of sleep and dreams must wane and give way to the tasks at hand. The first round of baguettes, focaccia, croissants, and morning buns are loaded into the ovens at 3:30. No conversation takes place at all. The only sounds to be heard are the walk-in and oven doors opening and closing, pastry racks being carted to and from the bake room, the hiss of the steam injector filling the oven chamber, and the bread loader rolling over the hot stone hearth. There are none of the typical distractions of the workplace—no phones are ringing, no calls to be made, nor errands to run or appointments to attend. Their labors are strictly shaping, mixing, and baking.

By 4 A.M. the thin crusts of a first batch of baguettes can be heard gently shattering (or "performing the bread song") as they cool. Two dozen pans of hot morning buns and croissants fill the bake room with a mesmerizing fusion of aromas: butter, cinnamon, brown sugar, and chocolate. The steam and heat of the deck oven along with the smells of fresh bread and pastry give one the sense of being in the safest place imaginable.

At 5 A.M. it is officially morning. Sunlight pours in through the southeast facing windows and seagulls can be heard from over the wharfs across Commercial Street as the retail and delivery staff arrive. There is more conversation now as everyone settles into their duties. All the while the baking continues. Cooling racks are almost overflowing and sheet pans of scones and more croissants seem to come out of the convection ovens exponentially faster. Cooled loaves are bagged for delivery and arranged on the retail display. Fresh pots of coffee begin to brew.

At 7 A.M. we open our doors and the first customers, the earliest risers, come inside. This space which was so dark and quiet only a few hours ago, is buzzing with all of the activity of a normal day. Feeling a sense of satisfaction and pride, the bakers watch people arriving and enjoying the fruits of their labor.

Matt James

TARTS

Tarts can be intricate compositions with multiple layers or more humble combinations of butter pastry and fruit preserves. All sorts of fillings, including jams, fresh fruits, and nuts are perfectly balanced by thin, crisp pastry. As with all our recipes, we lean toward a more natural presentation, much like what you might see in a farmer's market. Our tarts are made to be eaten on the same day they're baked.

The tarts on our pastry counter reflect and change with the seasons, from rhubarb in late spring to raspberries and blueberries to gorgeous peaches and nectarines in the peak of summer. When the air turns crisp in September, the first local apple varieties appear in the farmers' markets and our apple tart season begins. In late fall we turn to dried and preserved fruits, nuts, and chocolate as the supply of fresh fruit begins to wane.

My favorite of all of these recipes is the Rustic Apple Tart (page 74). To me there is nothing better than this quintessential marriage of flaky, buttery pastry with juicy fresh fruit. The hand-formed pastry leaving a portion of the fruit exposed to the heat of the oven, slightly charring the tips. The fruit-to-pastry ratio is in perfect balance, like a somewhat refined cousin of the American pie.

Most of our tarts use our Sweet Tart Dough (page 161), its fine crumbly texture similar to shortbread. For the richest flavor, we bake our tart shells to a distinctive dark golden brown. It not only brings out the nuttiness of the butter but also looks much more beautiful than a pale, under-baked crust. In the bakery we make 3-inch tarts, but most of the recipes in here have been converted to 9-inch tarts, which make 6 to 8 servings.

ALMOND RASPBERRY GALETTE

A thin layer of raspberry jam lends a tangy counterpoint to this classic buttery pastry, made all the richer with ground almonds. In France this dough is known as sablé, its sandy texture making it a close relative of shortbread cookies. I learned to make this version from Philippe LeCorre when he taught at the National Baking Center in Minneapolis. Baked a few extra minutes to a deep caramel finish, this tart is exactly what you would see in the window of a Parisian boulangerie. If you don't have a tart ring, you could also use a 2-inch-tall cake ring or a springform pan. A.P. *MAKES ONE 8-INCH TART*

1 CUP (2 STICKS) UNSALTED BUTTER, SOFTENED

2 CUPS ALL-PURPOSE FLOUR

PINCH SALT

¾ CUP SUGAR

⅓ CUP ALMOND MEAL

¼ CUP EGG, BEATEN

⅔ CUP RASPBERRY JAM

For the egg wash:

1 EGG

PINCH SALT

1. In the bowl of a stand mixer fitted with the paddle attachment, mix the butter, flour, and salt on low speed until well incorporated. Add the sugar and almond meal, beating until combined. Add the egg and mix just until the dough holds together and cleans the sides of the bowl.

2. Transfer the dough to a lightly floured work surface. With the heel of your hand, smear the pastry against the surface by pressing it down and away from you, working roughly 2-inch sections of dough at a time. This final step, called *fraisage*, helps to incorporate the butter into the flour.

3. Scrape the dough up with a plastic scraper and gather it into a mass. Divide it into two sections and form each into a smooth ball. Wrap 1 section with plastic wrap, flatten it into a disc, and place it in the refrigerator while you begin assembling the tart.

4. Lightly grease an 8-inch tart ring and place it on a parchment-lined baking sheet. To make the egg wash, in a small bowl beat the egg, 2 teaspoons of water, and salt together with a fork until smooth.

5. On a lightly floured work surface, roll half of the dough to a thickness of about ¼ inch. Fit the dough into the bottom of the tart ring and press the dough out with your hands until it fills the ring.

6. Using a pastry brush, brush the outside edge of the pastry with a 1-inch-wide border of the egg wash. Spread the jam uniformly over the dough within the egg wash border.

7. Remove the other half of the dough from the refrigerator (it should be slightly chilled but not firm), unwrap it and place it on a lightly floured work surface. Roll it out to about ¼-inch thick and place it on top of the raspberry jam, making sure it sits inside the tart ring. Lightly press the dough along the edges to firmly seal the two layers.

8. Brush the surface of the dough with a thin coat of egg wash. Chill the galette for about 10 to 15 minutes to relax the dough and firm the surface before scoring it.

9. Position a rack in the middle of the oven and preheat the oven to 350 degrees.

10. Remove the tart from the refrigerator, and using a fork, seal the edge of the galette by pressing the tines of the fork onto the surface of the dough all around the border. Using the fork or the dull side of a table knife, score a lattice pattern on the surface of the dough, or use any decorative pattern that you like.

11. Bake for 40 minutes or until golden brown, rotating the pan halfway through the baking time.

12. Remove from the oven. For a glossy, deeply caramelized finish, increase the oven temperature to 500 degrees. Sift confectioners' sugar lightly over the top of the galette and return it to the hot oven for 5 to 6 minutes or until most of the sugar has melted and the pastry has turned a rich mahogany color.

13. Remove from the oven and place on a wire rack. While the galette is still slightly warm, gently lift and remove the tart ring. If it is stuck, slide a knife between the pastry and the ring, then try twisting it side to side to loosen it before lifting it up and off the tart, being careful to avoid pulling up the top layer of pastry and separating it from the bottom.

BITTERSWEET TRUFFLE TARTELETTE

What could be more tempting than a crisp chocolate tart shell filled with rich chocolate ganache! This tart is the little black dress of your dessert repertoire. It is ready for accessories. Spoon some raspberry jam or caramel sauce in the bottom, top with toasted nuts, sliced strawberries, or fresh whipped cream. I occasionally go casual with some crushed pretzels and a bit of peanut butter. Spread a thin layer of fruit preserves or any addition of your choice, if using, on the tart shell before pouring in the ganache T.S. *MAKES SIX 4-INCH TARTELETTES*

SIX 4-INCH CHOCOLATE TART DOUGH SHELLS, FULLY BAKED AND COOLED (PAGES 157-158)
1 CUP (5.5 OUNCES) FINELY CHOPPED BITTERSWEET CHOCOLATE
½ CUP HALF-AND-HALF

1. Place the chopped chocolate in a medium bowl.

2. Bring the half-and-half to just a boil in a small saucepan. Pour over the chocolate and stir until the mixture is smooth.

3. Pour the chocolate into a measuring cup with a pour spout to make filling the tart shells easier.

4. Carefully pour the warm chocolate into the shells, filling nearly to the top. Refrigerate until the filling is set and firm, at least 30 minutes.

5. When the chocolate is set, top with any optional garnish, and serve. It's best to remove from the refrigerator for about 30 minutes before serving for the best flavor and texture.

CARAMEL APPLE TARTELETTE

This tart gave me my first "Proust's Madeleine" experience. The sweet, buttery, and slightly spicy flavor instantly sent me back to my childhood. It is reminiscent of the fried apple pies, crispy and rolled in cinnamon sugar, that I loved growing up. When I brought one to my husband, Chris, I saw the same sparks of recognition in his eyes. It is his favorite of all my creations. So far... T.S.

The tart dough, apple filling, Caramel Sauce and Streusel can be made and refrigerated up to 2 days ahead of time. The apple filling and caramel should be brought to room temperature before filling the tart molds. *MAKES 12 TARTELETTES*

1 RECIPE PERFECT TART DOUGH, CHILLED (PAGES 158-159)
1 RECIPE CARAMEL SAUCE (PAGE 160)

For the apple filling:
6 CUPS PEELED, CORED, AND SLICED TART APPLES (ABOUT 5 MEDIUM-SIZE APPLES)
¾ CUP SUGAR
1 TEASPOON LEMON JUICE
¼ TEASPOON GROUND CINNAMON
⅛ TEASPOON GROUND ALLSPICE
⅛ TEASPOON GROUND CLOVES
PINCH SALT

1½ CUPS STREUSEL (PAGE 170)

To make the apple filling:

1. Place the apples, sugar, lemon juice, cinnamon, allspice, cloves, salt, and ½ cup of water in a large saucepan and toss together. Simmer over medium-low heat until the apples soften and begin to fall apart and the liquid reduces. This should take 1½ to 2 hours. Use a spoon to break up and crush any large apple pieces remaining. The filling should resemble a chunky applesauce. Set aside to cool.

To roll out and shape the tart dough:

1. Remove one disc of tart dough from the refrigerator.

2. With a rolling pin, roll out the tart dough on a lightly floured surface to ⅛-inch-thick, using flour as needed to prevent the dough from sticking to the table and rolling pin.

3. Allow the dough to rest for a few minutes before cutting to prevent the dough circles from shrinking afterwards.

4. Cut the dough into six 5-inch circles and line six cups in a 12-cup muffin tin with the dough. Press the dough firmly into the cups and flatten out any folds ensuring an even thickness around the edge.

5. Remove the second disc of tart dough from the refrigerator and repeat steps 2 through 4. Refrigerate the tart shells in the muffin tin for at least one hour.

To fill and bake the tarts:

1. Position a rack in the center of the oven and preheat the oven to 375 degrees. Remove the prepared tart shells from the refrigerator.

2. Spoon about a tablespoon of the cooled caramel sauce into the bottom of each chilled tart shell.

3. Fill the shells with the apple filling leaving a ½-inch border at the top. Top the apple filling with a heaping ⅛ cup streusel.

4. Place a sheet of aluminum foil under the pan on the oven rack to catch any filling that may boil out. Bake the tarts for 23 to 24 minutes, rotating the pan half way through the baking time. The pastry is done when the tart dough is lightly browned and all translucency is gone.

5. Remove from the oven and place on a wire rack for about 10 minutes before removing the tarts. A small offset spatula or a knife works well to pull the tart out. Finish cooling the tarts directly on the wire rack or serve while still warm.

> *It is reminiscent of fried apple pies, crispy and rolled in cinnamon sugar.*

CHOCOLATE PECAN TART

As simple and pleasing as a candy bar with layers of buttery caramel, bittersweet chocolate, and toasted pecans, yet refined enough for celebrations. This tart is the epitome of an ultra rich and sweet extravagance that will definitely give you the feeling of indulgence. This is a good choice when entertaining as this lavish dessert is best served in thin slices. You could also substitute toasted walnuts for the pecans. *MAKES ONE 9-INCH TART*

ONE 9-INCH CHOCOLATE TART DOUGH SHELL, UNBAKED AND CHILLED (PAGES 157-158)

⅓ CUP PLUS 1 TABLESPOON CARAMEL SAUCE (PAGE 160)

¼ CUP PLUS 1 TABLESPOON SUGAR

1 EGG

½ TEASPOON SALT

2 TABLESPOONS UNSALTED BUTTER, MELTED AND COOLED

¼ CUP PLUS 1 TABLESPOON LIGHT CORN SYRUP

1½ TEASPOONS MOLASSES

1⅔ CUPS TOASTED PECANS, CRUSHED INTO LARGE IRREGULAR PIECES (SEE INSTRUCTIONS ON PAGE 170)

¼ CUP CHOPPED BITTERSWEET CHOCOLATE

To mix the filling:

1. In a medium bowl, whisk together the sugar and egg.

2. Add the salt, butter, corn syrup, and molasses and stir to combine.

To assemble and bake the tart:

1. Position a rack in the center of the oven and preheat the oven to 375 degrees.

2. In a medium bowl, with a wooden spoon stir to combine the caramel sauce, the filling, pecans, and chocolate.

3. Remove the tart shell from the refrigerator. Pour the mixture into the chilled tart shell, spreading the filling and pecan pieces out evenly.

4. Bake for 25 minutes, rotating the pan half way through the baking time. The filling should be puffed up slightly and lightly browned.

5. Remove from the oven and place the tart pan on a wire rack to cool completely. Serve at room temperature.

HAZELNUT CHOCOLATE TART

This elegant tart is one of our more elaborate holiday desserts. It it almost more of a confection than a tart. Garnished with flake sea salt, the flavors sing —and the contrast of the bright white flecks against the dark chocolate ganache is striking. We use Maldon sea salt, which has light textured flakes and a clean, salty flavor. The candied hazelnuts can be prepared up to one week before serving and stored in an airtight container.

The tart can be baked the day ahead, but needs to be glazed the day it is being served or the sugar will melt off the candied hazelnuts. *MAKES ONE 9-INCH TART*

ONE 9-INCH SWEET TART DOUGH SHELL, UNBAKED AND CHILLED (PAGE 161)

For the hazelnut filling:
½ CUP SUGAR
⅓ CUP MILK
4 TABLESPOONS (½ STICK) UNSALTED BUTTER
¼ TEASPOON VANILLA EXTRACT
⅛ TEASPOON SALT
1½ CUPS HAZELNUTS, TOASTED, SKINNED, AND FINELY CHOPPED (SEE INSTRUCTIONS ON PAGE 170)
¼ TEASPOON GROUND CINNAMON
1 EGG, BEATEN

For the apricot glaze:
2 TABLESPOONS SMOOTH APRICOT JAM

For the ganache:
⅔ CUP (3 OUNCES) FINELY CHOPPED BITTERSWEET CHOCOLATE
3 TABLESPOONS HALF-AND-HALF
12 CANDIED HAZELNUTS (PAGE 144)
FLAKE SEA SALT, FOR GARNISH

To make the hazelnut filling:

1. Combine the sugar, milk, butter, vanilla, and salt in a small saucepan. Bring the mixture to a boil over medium heat.

2. Remove the pan from heat and add the chopped hazelnuts and cinnamon. Stir to combine and set aside to cool.

3. When the mixture is completely cool, stir in the egg.

To bake the tart:

1. Position a rack in the center of the oven and preheat the oven to 375 degrees.

2. Remove the tart shell from the refrigerator. Pour the filling into the chilled tart shell and smooth it evenly over the bottom with a small offset spatula.

3. Bake for 35 minutes, rotating the pan half way through the baking time. The tart shell should be browned and the filling firm. Place the tart pan on a cooling rack and cool completely before glazing.

To finish the tart:

1. To make the apricot glaze, warm the apricot jam and 1 tablespoon of water together in a small saucepan over low heat, until melted and heated through. Remove it from the heat.

2. Pour the warm apricot glaze over the top of the cooled tart and spread it with a small offset spatula.

3. To make the chocolate ganache, place the finely chopped bittersweet chocolate in a small heatproof bowl. Pour the half-and-half into a small saucepan and heat to a boil. Remove from the heat and pour it over the chocolate. Stir until smooth.

4. Pour the ganache over the apricot glaze and spread it evenly over the surface. Place the candied hazelnuts decoratively around the outside edge of the tart. Sprinkle a pinch of flake sea salt over the ganache to garnish.

[
This is more of a confection than a tart.
]

CHOCOLATE IRISH CREAM TART

The inspiration for this tart came from a *Bon Appetit* recipe from 1999. We had wanted to make something special for the St. Patrick's Day celebration. Our little pastry became a superstar, having us looking forward to this holiday treat in the middle of an otherwise uneventful month. Our adaptation of this recipe is an extra-deep flaky tart shell filled with a dark, melty chocolate filling with a whiskey kick. The Irish cream ganache and chocolate shavings dress this tart up for a dinner party dessert plate.

Note: To make chocolate shavings, place a bar or block of high-quality chocolate in the refrigerator for about 10 minutes. Place a piece of parchment paper or foil over your work surface to collect the shavings. Use a folded paper towel to wrap around the bar to prevent the chocolate from melting as you work. Hold the chocolate in one hand and firmly scrape the edge of the chocolate with a vegetable peeler in one fluid motion. *MAKES 12 TARTELETTES*

1 RECIPE PERFECT TART DOUGH, CHILLED FOR AT LEAST 4 HOURS (PAGES 158-159)

For the chocolate filling:

1 CUP PLUS ¼ CUP CHOPPED BITTERSWEET CHOCOLATE

⅛ CUP WHISKEY

1 TEASPOON VANILLA EXTRACT

¾ TEASPOON INSTANT ESPRESSO POWDER

PINCH SALT

3 EGGS, SEPARATED

⅓ CUP SUGAR

For the ganache:

3 TABLESPOONS IRISH CREAM LIQUOR

¾ CUP CHOPPED WHITE CHOCOLATE

¼ CUP (½ STICK) BUTTER, SOFTENED

BITTERSWEET CHOCOLATE SHAVINGS, FOR GARNISH

To partially bake the tart shells:

1. Roll out the tart dough to ⅛-inch thick and let it rest a few minutes before cutting. Cut the dough into 5½-inch circles. Line brioche molds or a 12-cup muffin tin with the tart dough. The dough should extend up above the rim by about ¼ inch. Refrigerate for 1 hour.

2. Position a rack in the center of the oven and preheat the oven to 400 degrees.

3. Use a fork to pierce the bottom of each tart shell. Cut parchment paper into 6-inch squares and press into the molds over the tart dough. Fill to the very top with dried beans.

4. Bake for 10 minutes. Carefully remove the parchment and beans. Use a fork to press out any bubbles in the dough that have puffed up from the bottom or sides of the tin. Bake for an additional 3 minutes. Set the shells aside to cool in the tins.

To make the chocolate filling:

1. Set aside the ¼ cup of chocolate. Place the remaining chocolate in a medium bowl set over a pot of simmering water. Stir until the chocolate is completely melted. Remove the bowl from the heat.

2. Whisk in the whiskey. The mixture will be stiff initially, but will become smooth as you continue whisking. Whisk in the vanilla, espresso powder, salt, and yolks. Set aside.

3. In the bowl of a stand mixer fitted with the whisk attachment, beat the egg whites on medium speed until they are frothy and opaque.

4. Gradually add the sugar, beating until the whites are stiff enough to hold a peak when you lift the whisk out of the mixture.

5. Gently fold ¼ of the egg whites into the chocolate mixture with a rubber spatula. Fold in half of the remaining whites, then the reserved ¼ cup chopped chocolate, followed by the remaining whites.

6. Spoon the filling into the prepared tart shells, filling them ½ inch from the top. Place the filled tarts in the freezer for 2 hours, until firm.

To make the ganache:

1. In a small saucepan, heat the Irish cream to a boil. Remove the pan from the heat and stir in the white chocolate. When the chocolate is melted and the mixture is smooth, transfer to a small bowl and set aside to cool.

2. When the mixture is completely cool, whisk in the butter. Refrigerate for about 5 minutes, remove from the refrigerator, and whisk again. Repeat in this manner, whisking until the ganache is light and creamy. Set it aside at room temperature.

Baking and finishing the tarts:

1. Position a rack in the center of the oven and preheat the oven to 350 degrees. Line a baking sheet with parchment paper.

2. Carefully remove the tarts from the tins and place them on a baking sheet.

3. Bake for 8 minutes, rotate the baking sheet, and bake for an additional 8 minutes. The filling will have puffed up and started to crack.

4. Carefully slide the parchment paper off the baking sheet and onto a wire rack. Cool the tarts completely.

5. Spoon about a tablespoon of the ganache on each tart. A small cookie scoop or a piping bag can be used for a more decorative look. Garnish with chocolate shavings and serve.

FRUIT AND CREAM CHEESE TART

This tart brings to mind a fruit-topped cheesecake, but lighter and with the fruit as the focus. Our versatile recipe showcases your homemade fruit preserves, blanketing them with a lavish layer of cream cheese and crumbly streusel. You can find some excellent home-style preserves in specialty food stores. Select one with pieces of fruit and all-natural ingredients. In the bakery, we make a cherry compote, but strawberry or blueberry would also be classic flavor combinations. *MAKES ONE 9-INCH TART*

ONE 9-INCH PERFECT TART DOUGH SHELL, PARTIALLY BAKED AND COOLED (PAGES 158-159)
1 CUP FRUIT PRESERVES
1 RECIPE CREAM CHEESE FILLING, AT ROOM TEMPERATURE (PAGE 167)
1 RECIPE STREUSEL (PAGE 170)

1. Position a rack in the center of the oven and preheat the oven to 350 degrees.

2. Using a small off-set spatula, spread the preserves evenly over the bottom of the tart shell.

3. Spoon the cream cheese filling over the fruit. Use a small off-set spatula to smooth the filling into a uniform layer.

4. Crumble the streusel over the cream cheese filling, covering the entire top.

5. Bake for 40 minutes, rotating the pan half way through the baking time. The streusel and the crust should be golden brown and crisp.

6. Remove from the oven and transfer the pan to a wire rack. Serve at room temperature.

LEMON TART

This unusual filling uses the whole lemon—juice, pulp, and zest, almost like a lemon jam. At first we were skeptical about using the whole fruit, but were immediately won over by the lively punch of citrus. The sharp lemon tang is mellowed perfectly by the sweet pastry crust. This tart makes an elegant dessert, or as an accompaniment to coffee or tea, it satisfies those late afternoon cravings for something just a little bit sweet. *MAKES ONE 9-INCH TART*

ONE 9-INCH SWEET TART DOUGH SHELL, UNBAKED AND CHILLED (PAGE 161)

1 MEDIUM LEMON

1½ CUPS SUGAR

1 TABLESPOON PLUS 1 TEASPOON CORNSTARCH

1 EGG

1 EGG YOLK

7 TABLESPOONS UNSALTED BUTTER, MELTED AND COOLED

1. Position a rack in the center of the oven and preheat the oven to 365 degrees.

2. Wash the lemon and wipe it dry with a towel. In a small bowl, whisk together the sugar and cornstarch.

3. On a cutting board, cut off the ends of the lemon. Cut the lemon into quarters lengthwise. Remove any visible seeds. Slice each quarter into ⅛-inch pieces, removing any additional seeds you come across.

4. In a medium bowl, toss the lemon slices with the sugar mixture. Transfer this mixture to a food processor fitted with the blade attachment and blend until the lemon mixture is nearly smooth, with only very small pieces remaining, 30 to 60 seconds.

5. Add the egg, yolk, and melted butter to the food processor and pulse once or twice until everything is combined.

6. Remove the tart shell from the refrigerator. Pour the lemon filling into the chilled tart shell. Bake the tart for 40 to 45 minutes, rotating the pan halfway through the baking time. The crust should be well-baked and golden brown, the surface bubbly and speckled with dark brown spots.

7. Remove from the oven and cool completely on a wire rack. Serve at room temperature.

BLUEBERRY LEMON TART

The apricot glaze helps to hold the berries in place and to retain their moisture. Alternatively, you could omit the glaze and instead lightly dust the fruit topping with confectioners' sugar for a decorative touch. *MAKES ONE 9-INCH TART*

ONE 9-INCH LEMON TART, BAKED AND COOLED

2 TABLESPOONS SMOOTH APRICOT JAM, FOR GLAZE

2 CUPS (1 PINT) BLUEBERRIES (STRAWBERRIES, RASPBERRIES, OR ANY OTHER FRESH SEASONAL BERRY CAN BE SUBSTITUTED)

1. In a small saucepan over low heat, warm the apricot jam and 1 tablespoon of water together until melted and heated through. Remove it from the heat.

2. In a large bowl, toss the blueberries with the warm apricot glaze, being careful to avoid damaging the surface of the fruit.

3. Gently scoop the berries out of the bowl and pile them decoratively on top of the lemon tart.

PEACH BROWN BUTTER STREUSEL TART

This tart is one of the many ways that we showcase seasonal fruit. We start the year with rhubarb, and spend the summer with peaches, nectarines, and plums. We make a cranberry orange compote for the winter months. The sweet, buttery streusel is a perfect accompaniment to fruit that has a bit of tartness. Taste the fruit you are using to determine how much sugar to add. If you are using ripe, sweet fruit, add the smaller amount. Use the larger amount if you have tart or slightly under-ripe fruit that needs more sweetness. *MAKES ONE 9-INCH TART*

ONE 9-INCH SWEET TART DOUGH SHELL, PARTIALLY BAKED AND COOLED (PAGE 161)

¼ TO ½ CUP SUGAR

⅛ CUP ALL-PURPOSE FLOUR

½ TEASPOON GROUND CINNAMON

2½ CUPS DICED RIPE PEACHES (ABOUT 3 MEDIUM), NECTARINES, OR PLUMS

ZEST FROM ONE LEMON

1 RECIPE BROWN BUTTER STREUSEL (PAGE 169)

CONFECTIONERS' SUGAR FOR DUSTING

1. Position a rack in the center of the oven and preheat the oven to 375 degrees.

2. In a large bowl, combine the sugar, flour, and cinnamon.

3. Add the diced peaches and lemon zest and toss until the fruit is evenly coated with the sugar mixture.

4. Spoon the fruit into the prepared tart shell and spread it evenly over the bottom.

5. Crumble the streusel over the fruit and carefully spread it to the edges of the tart, completely covering the fruit. The fruit and streusel will be higher than the edge of the tart shell but it will reduce as it bakes.

6. Bake for 30 minutes, carefully rotating the pan half way through the bake time. The streusel and the tart shell should be deep brown in color.

7. Remove from the oven and cool on a wire rack.

8. Garnish the tart with a dusting of confectioners' sugar before serving.

RHUBARB BROWN BUTTER STREUSEL TART

In Maine, rhubarb is the first fruit of the growing season. All winter long we anticipate the arrival date of this tart, juicy summer fruit, until we can begin baking these lovely tarts. *MAKES ONE 9-INCH TART*

ONE 9-INCH SWEET TART DOUGH SHELL, PARTIALLY BAKED AND COOLED (PAGE 161)
½ CUP SUGAR
⅛ CUP ALL-PURPOSE FLOUR
2½ CUPS DICED RHUBARB
ZEST OF 1 LEMON
1 RECIPE BROWN BUTTER STREUSEL (PAGE 169)
CONFECTIONERS' SUGAR FOR DUSTING

1. To make the rhubarb filling, combine the sugar and flour in a large bowl.

2. Add the diced rhubarb and lemon zest and toss until the fruit is evenly coated with the sugar mixture.

3. Follow the recipe above from step 4.

PEAR FRANGIPANE TART

The combination of fresh poached pears and sweet, nutty frangipane is delightful. This is one of our most popular holiday desserts, as well as a regular feature of our fall/winter pastry offerings. The pear flavor is improved by sitting overnight in the syrup and can be made up to a week ahead of time. Fresh plums, apricots, and tart cherries also pair beautifully with the almond frangipane and become the starlets of our pastry display when in season. *MAKES ONE 9-INCH TART*

ONE 9-INCH SWEET TART DOUGH SHELL, UNBAKED AND CHILLED (PAGE 161)
1 RECIPE FRANGIPANE (PAGE 168)
8 POACHED PEAR HALVES, DRAINED, (PAGE 171) OR OTHER FRUIT
2 TABLESPOONS SMOOTH APRICOT JAM, FOR GLAZE

1. Position a rack in the center of the oven and preheat the oven to 350 degrees. Line a baking sheet with parchment paper.

2. To dry the pears, place them on a paper towel and dab them to remove excess syrup. On a cutting board, place a pear half cut side down. While holding the pear together, slice it crosswise into ¼-inch slices. Repeat with the rest of the pear halves.

3. Remove the tart shell from the refrigerator and place it on the baking sheet. Using a rubber or offset spatula, spread the frangipane uniformly in the shell.

4. Pick up each pear half and fan the slices out, then place it on the frangipane with the narrow end towards the center. Fan the rest of the pear halves in the same manner and evenly space them on the top of the frangipane with their narrow ends almost meeting in the center

5. Bake for 40 minutes, rotating the baking sheet half way through the baking time, until the crust is golden brown and the filling is set. The filling should feel firm to the touch and slightly springy. The fruit should be browning slightly around the edges.

6. Remove the tart from the oven and transfer it to a wire rack to cool slightly.

7. While the tart is cooling, prepare the apricot glaze: In a small saucepan over low heat, warm the apricot jam and 1 tablespoon of water together until melted and heated through. Remove it from the heat. With a pastry brush, brush the glaze over the fruit while the tart is still warm.

8. To unmold the tart, place it on a bowl or other object that is smaller in diameter than the tart pan and the ring will slip off. Serve warm or at room temperature.

APRICOT FRANGIPANE TART

Golden sweet apricots are a perfect choice for this tart. Choose ripe but still firm apricots for the best results. *MAKES ONE 9-INCH TART*

ONE 9-INCH SWEET TART DOUGH SHELL, UNBAKED AND CHILLED (PAGE 161)

4 RIPE APRICOTS

1 RECIPE FRANGIPANE (PAGE 168)

2 TABLESPOONS SMOOTH APRICOT JAM, FOR GLAZE

1. Position a rack in the center of the oven and preheat the oven to 350 degrees. Line a baking sheet with parchment paper.

2. Remove the tart shell from the refrigerator and place it on the baking sheet. Using a rubber or offset spatula, spread the frangipane uniformly in the shell.

3. Cut the apricots in half and remove the pits. Slice the apricot halves into ¼-inch slices and arrange decoratively on top of the frangipane, fanning the slices from the center to the edge.

4. Continue following the recipe from step 5.

CHERRY FRANGIPANE TART

We tried many varieties of canned and fresh cherries before finding the perfect ones. We found that canned cherries kept their moisture and baked beautifully without falling apart. Look for tart cherries packed in water or juice, not syrup. *MAKES ONE 9-INCH TART*

ONE 9-INCH SWEET TART DOUGH SHELL, UNBAKED AND CHILLED (PAGE 161)

ONE 14.5 OUNCE CAN TART CHERRIES IN WATER, DRAINED

1 RECIPE FRANGIPANE (PAGE 168)

2 TABLESPOONS SMOOTH APRICOT JAM, FOR GLAZE

1. Position a rack in the center of the oven and preheat the oven to 350 degrees. Line a baking sheet with parchment paper.

2. Remove the tart shell from the refrigerator and place it on the baking sheet. Using a rubber or offset spatula, spread the frangipane uniformly in the shell.

3. Arrange the drained cherries evenly over the frangipane.

4. Continue following the recipe from step 5.

PLUM FRANGIPANE TART

The beautiful crimson color of ripe plums makes this tart a showstopper. Black plums are our favorite at the bakery because of the deep red flesh and sweet flavor. We also like to use red plums, which have a pleasing contrast of dark peel and golden fruit. Most importantly, the fruit should be at its peak of ripeness. *MAKES ONE 9-INCH TART*

ONE 9-INCH SWEET TART DOUGH SHELL, UNBAKED AND CHILLED (PAGE 161)

3 RIPE PLUMS

1 RECIPE FRANGIPANE (PAGE 168)

2 TABLESPOONS SMOOTH APRICOT JAM, FOR GLAZE

1. Position a rack in the center of the oven and preheat the oven to 350 degrees. Line a baking sheet with parchment paper.

2. Remove the tart shell from the refrigerator and place it on the baking sheet. Using a rubber or offset spatula, spread the frangipane uniformly in the shell.

3. Cut the plums in half and remove the pits. Slice the plum halves into ¼-inch thick slices and arrange decoratively on the top of the frangipane, fanning the slices out from the center to the edge.

4. Continue following the recipe from step 5.

[
The beautiful crimson color of ripe plums makes this tart a showstopper.
]

RUSTIC APPLE TART

This beautiful tart has lovely folds of flaky, buttery dough enveloping a mound of fresh seasonal fruit. A sprinkle of streusel adds the final touch. This lovely pastry conjures up images of a farmhouse lunch table in the height of harvest time. We love substituting plums for the apples in the summer. Amazing flavor and a gorgeous crimson color! And just think...no pie pan to wash!

When properly made, the apple slices will retain their shape after baking, but be very tender, not firm or crisp. Depending on the variety and freshness of your apples, the fruit may need to be sliced thinner or wider to achieve the desired texture. *MAKES ONE 8-INCH TART OR FOUR 4-INCH TARTS*

1 RECIPE RUSTIC TART DOUGH, ROLLED OUT AND CHILLED (PAGE 162)
4 MEDIUM (ABOUT 1½ POUNDS) APPLES (GRAVENSTEIN OR OTHER TART BAKING VARIETY)
¼ CUP SUGAR
2 TABLESPOONS ALL-PURPOSE FLOUR
½ TEASPOON GROUND CINNAMON
⅛ TEASPOON FRESHLY GRATED NUTMEG
1 CUP STREUSEL (PAGE 170)

For the egg wash:
1 EGG
PINCH SALT

1. Position a rack in the center of the oven and preheat the oven to 425 degrees. Line a baking sheet with parchment paper.

2. In a small bowl, make the egg wash by beating the egg, 2 teaspoons of water, and salt with a fork.

3. In a large bowl, combine the sugar, flour, cinnamon, and nutmeg.

4. Peel, core, and slice the apples into ½-inch-thick slices. Toss the apples in the spice mixture until the slices are evenly coated. Remove the small circles of tart dough from the refrigerator and place them on a lightly floured work surface. If you are making a large tart, place the large tart circle on the prepared baking sheet. Use a pastry brush to egg wash around the outside inch of the tart circles.

5. Divide the apples among the four small tarts, piling them in the center, leaving a 2-inch border around the edge. For the large tart, pile the apples into the center, leaving a 3-inch border around the edge.

6. For small tarts, fold a 3-inch portion of the dough over the apples, fold the next 3 inches up,

overlapping the last portion by an inch. Continue to fold the dough up around the apples until you overlap the first fold. Place tarts evenly spaced on the prepared baking sheet. For a large tart, fold up using 4-inch folds.

7. Lightly brush the outside surface of the tart with the egg wash. Top each small tart with ¼ cup of streusel, gently squeezing and pressing it into the tart to hold it in place. Top the large tart with 1 cup of streusel.

8. Bake both the large and small tarts for 10 minutes, rotate the baking sheet, and reduce the oven temperature to 375 degrees. Bake the small tarts for another 25 minutes. Bake the large tart for another 35 minutes, or until the pastry is a dark golden brown and the folds of tart dough no longer have a translucent appearance.

9. Remove from the oven and carefully slide the parchment paper off of the baking sheet and onto a wire rack. Serve warm from the oven with creme fraiche, whipped cream, or ice cream. If serving at room temperature, cool completely on the wire rack.

RUSTIC PLUM TART

5 MEDIUM (ABOUT 1½ POUNDS) RIPE PLUMS

¼ CUP SUGAR

3 TABLESPOONS ALL-PURPOSE FLOUR

½ TEASPOON GROUND CINNAMON

Follow the recipe for the rustic apple tart, substituting plums that have been pitted and cut into 1-inch-thick slices.

RUSTIC PEACH TART

4 MEDIUM (ABOUT 1½ POUNDS) RIPE PEACHES

¼ CUP SUGAR

3 TABLESPOONS ALL-PURPOSE FLOUR

½ TEASPOON GROUND CINNAMON

Follow the recipe for the rustic apple tart substituting peaches that have been pitted and cut into 1-inch-thick slices.

CAKES

Our cakes tend to be homey, rustic affairs. Since we don't have a refrigerated pastry case in the bakery, multi-tiered cakes with layers of cream fillings wouldn't survive long before melting into puddles. Whipped cream and pastry creams are usually out of the question.

We prefer simple combinations of flours, ground nuts, fruits, and plenty of sweet butter. Never overly sweet, we look for a perfect balance of flavors. Most of our cakes are made in petite sizes of various shapes.

Our most popular cake is undoubtedly the Chocolate Cork. Based on the little French cakes seen in Parisian bakeries, we created a moist version embellished with a dusting of dark cocoa. The diminutive size packs an intense chocolate hit.

For me, however, the most perfect expression of a cake is probably the pound cake. Its firm, moist, buttery crumb creates an ideal background for just about any flavor additions. Our Blueberry Ricotta Custard Cake flies out of the bakery and elicits more comments than just about anything on our menu.

The Mediterranean Lemon Cake and Gingerbread are simple to put together and make great companions to various garnishes. The lemon cake lends itself to raspberry or other fruit purees, the gingerbread can be sliced and served with warm sautéed apples or pears, or just a dollop of freshly whipped cream.

We've also included bread pudding in this section, which we make with leftover brioche and croissants in the bakery. The spicy pumpkin filling is ideal for a cold winter day treat and makes an interesting twist on the traditional holiday pumpkin pie. I like to indulge myself with a warm slice drizzled with heavy cream—the ultimate creamy comfort food.

BROWNIES

Everyone thinks brownies are only about fudgy or cakey. We think this is the best brownie ever. Voluptuous 70% Callebaut, an ideal quantity of cocoa, folded into fresh eggs, butter, and sugar at just the right moment to create the elusive, shiny, paper-thin finish we longed for. *MAKES ABOUT 15 BROWNIES*

1½ CUPS ALL-PURPOSE FLOUR

⅓ CUP PLUS 2 TABLESPOONS DUTCH-PROCESSED COCOA POWDER

¾ TEASPOON BAKING POWDER

¾ TEASPOON SALT

2½ TEASPOONS INSTANT ESPRESSO POWDER

1½ CUPS (7 OUNCES) CHOPPED UNSWEETENED CHOCOLATE

⅓ CUP (1½ OUNCES) CHOPPED BITTERSWEET CHOCOLATE

1⅓ CUPS (2⅔ STICKS) UNSALTED BUTTER, PLUS EXTRA FOR GREASING PAN

5 EGGS, ROOM TEMPERATURE

3 CUPS SUGAR

2½ TEASPOONS VANILLA EXTRACT

1. Position a rack in the center of the oven and preheat the oven to 350 degrees. Spray a 9 x 13-inch pan with nonstick cooking spray or lightly grease with butter.

2. In a medium bowl, whisk together the flour, cocoa powder, baking powder, salt, and espresso powder.

3. In a medium saucepan, melt the unsweetened chocolate, bittersweet chocolate, and butter together over low heat. Set the pan aside to cool slightly.

4. In a large bowl, whisk the eggs just until smooth, then add the sugar and vanilla and whisk until combined.

5. Whisk the warm chocolate mixture into the egg mixture. Using a rubber spatula, fold the dry ingredients into the chocolate and egg mixture.

6. Pour the batter into the prepared pan and level with a spatula.

7. Bake for 38 to 40 minutes, rotating the pan after 20 minutes. The top will be crisp and a tester inserted in the center will come out with moist crumbs.

8. Remove the pan from the oven and place it on a wire rack until cooled completely.

9. To serve, cut into 2½ x 3-inch bars using a sharp knife. For cleaner edges you can dip the knife in hot water before slicing. Wipe the blade with a clean towel after each cut and repeat.

BLUEBERRY RICOTTA CUSTARD CAKE

This pound cake is made with extra creamy ricotta cheese. Ricotta adds an incredibly rich flavor and texture to the cake—reminiscent of vanilla custard. This moist, delicate cake complements the sweet-tart flavor of our locally grown Maine blueberries perfectly. Its flavor and texture improve overnight. Look for an Italian-style ricotta with a high fat content. It is thicker and creamier than American versions. *MAKES ONE 9-INCH LOAF*

1½ CUPS CAKE FLOUR, SIFTED, PLUS EXTRA FOR DUSTING PAN

2½ TEASPOONS BAKING POWDER

1 TEASPOON SALT

½ TEASPOON FRESHLY GRATED NUTMEG

¾ CUP (10 TABLESPOONS) UNSALTED BUTTER, SOFTENED

1¼ CUPS SUGAR

1 CUP PLUS 3 TABLESPOONS WHOLE MILK RICOTTA

3 EGGS, ROOM TEMPERATURE

1 TEASPOON VANILLA EXTRACT

1½ CUPS FRESH OR FROZEN BLUEBERRIES

1. Position a rack in the center of the oven and preheat the oven to 350 degrees.

2. Spray a 9 x 5-inch loaf pan with nonstick cooking spray and dust with flour.

3. In a medium bowl, whisk together the flour, baking powder, salt, and nutmeg.

4. In the bowl of a stand mixer fitted with the paddle attachment, or using a hand mixer, cream together the softened butter and sugar until it is light and fluffy.

5. Gradually add the ricotta on medium-low speed until combined, occasionally scraping down the bowl with a rubber spatula to ensure there are no lumps and the mixture is smooth.

6. Begin adding the eggs one at a time. Scrape down the bowl between each egg addition. Add the vanilla.

7. Add the dry ingredients and mix on low speed until just combined. Scrape down the bowl again and mix on medium speed for about 30 seconds.

8. Carefully fold in the blueberries by hand with a rubber spatula. Be careful not to over mix because the blueberries will crush easily and stain the batter. Pour into the prepared loaf pan and smooth the top with the spatula.

9. Bake for 30 minutes. Gently rotate the pan and reduce the temperature to 325 degrees.

10. Bake for an additional 25 to 30 minutes. When done, the cake will be medium brown and a tester should come out clean when inserted in the center of the loaf.

11. Remove from the oven. Let the cake cool in the pan on a wire rack. After about 15 minutes, turn the cake out of the pan onto the rack to cool. This cake actually improves in flavor and texture overnight—so it is perfect to make the day before serving.

FLOURLESS CHOCOLATE CAKE

We serve this rustic chocolate cake for Passover every year. The cake will soufflé while baking, then sink as it cools. This creates a shallow bowl on top of the cake perfect for holding your favorite embellishments. It can be garnished with a layer of raspberry jam and chocolate shavings, freshly whipped cream, or a drizzle of chocolate ganache.

When whipping egg whites it's best to separate the eggs when cold, then bring the egg whites to room temperature before beating. Place the whites in a clean, dry bowl without any trace of yolks or grease and start beating on low speed. If beaten too quickly the structure of the foam will not be as strong. *MAKES ONE 9-INCH CAKE*

1¼ CUPS (6 OUNCES) CHOPPED BITTERSWEET CHOCOLATE
6 TABLESPOONS UNSALTED BUTTER
5 EGGS, SEPARATED, ROOM TEMPERATURE
PINCH SALT
⅓ CUP SUGAR
1½ TEASPOONS VANILLA EXTRACT
¾ CUP PLUS 2 TABLESPOONS ALMOND MEAL

1. In a small saucepan, melt the chocolate and butter together. Remove from the heat and allow to cool slightly.

2. Position a rack in the center of the oven and preheat the oven to 350 degrees. Grease a 9-inch springform pan with nonstick cooking spray.

3. In the bowl of a stand mixer fitted with the whisk attachment, whip the egg whites and salt, beginning on low speed and gradually increasing the speed to high until they become opaque and frothy.

4. Gradually add the sugar to the egg whites and continue whipping just until firm peaks are formed, being careful not to create stiff meringue. Transfer to another large bowl.

5. Wipe the bowl clean, then add the egg yolks and vanilla. Using the whisk attachment, whip the egg yolks and vanilla until pale, about 5 minutes on medium speed.

6. Fold the almond meal into the yolk mixture gently with a rubber spatula, bringing the batter from the bottom of the bowl gently over the top. Rotate the bowl as you continue to fold the mixture until combined. Then fold in the chocolate mixture and ¼ of the whites.

7. Gently fold in the remaining whites in two stages.

8. Pour the batter into the prepared pan and smooth the top gently with an offset spatula.

9. Bake for 25 to 30 minutes, rotating the pan half way through the baking time. The cake will feel airy yet set, when lightly touched on the top. It will fall slightly as it cools.

10. Remove from the oven and cool in the pan on a wire rack. After the cake has cooled slightly, run a knife between the side of the cake and the pan and remove the springform ring. Serve at room temperature with the garnish of your choice and freshly whipped cream.

> *It can be garnished with a layer of raspberry jam and chocolate shavings, freshly whipped cream, or a drizzle of chocolate ganache.*

CHOCOLATE CORKS

After tasting chocolate bouchon in bakeries all over Paris, we returned home intent on creating our own version of these rich, dense chocolate delights. While some bouchon tend to be dry, ours is very moist and not quite as firm as most. We use an extra dark cocoa, Cacao Barry Cocoa-Extra Brute, which imparts a deep, almost black color to these diminutive cakes. Since there is such a large percentage of cocoa in this recipe, you should seek out the best quality cocoa available. A.P.

Note: In the bakery we use 2¼-inch by 2¼-inch stainless steel cake rings. Kerekes Bakery & Restaurant Equipment (see Sources page 175) sells 2-inch cake rings and a large variety of timbale molds, baba cups, and silicone fleximolds that have a similar "cork" shape that can be used instead. Also, Chicago Metallic Bakeware makes a mini-popover pan that would be a great alternative. In a pinch, you could use a 6-cup muffin pan and make a short, wide cake instead of a cork.
MAKES 12 CORKS

For the cake:
½ CUP DUTCH-PROCESSED COCOA POWDER, PLUS MORE FOR DUSTING
¼ CUP PLUS 2 TABLESPOONS HOT WATER
3 EGGS, ROOM TEMPERATURE
1½ TEASPOONS VANILLA EXTRACT
1 CUP ALL-PURPOSE FLOUR
1 CUP PLUS 1 TABLESPOON PLUS 1 TEASPOON SUGAR
1 TEASPOON BAKING POWDER
PINCH SALT
13 TABLESPOONS UNSALTED BUTTER, ROOM TEMPERATURE
2¼ CUPS (12 OUNCES) CHOPPED BITTERSWEET CHOCOLATE

For the coffee syrup:
2 TABLESPOONS SUGAR
1 TEASPOON INSTANT ESPRESSO POWDER (OPTIONAL)
2 CUPS STRONG BREWED COFFEE

1. In a medium bowl or a glass measuring cup, stir together the sugar and espresso powder, if using. Then add the hot coffee. Set the syrup aside to cool.

2. Position a rack in the center of the oven and preheat the oven to 375 degrees. Line a baking sheet with parchment paper. Spray 12 cake molds with nonstick cooking spray or grease with butter.

3. In a medium bowl, stir together the cocoa powder and hot water to make a stiff paste. Add the eggs and vanilla and stir until combined (the mixture will be very lumpy).

4. In a medium bowl, whisk together the flour, sugar, baking powder, and salt.

5. In the bowl of a stand mixer fitted with the paddle attachment, beat the butter on medium speed until it's smooth. Add the dry ingredients and beat on medium speed until incorporated. Add the cocoa mixture and mix on low until dry ingredients are evenly moist.

6. Beat on medium speed for 1 minute to aerate the mixture. Scrape the sides of the bowl and paddle frequently.

7. On low speed, add the chopped chocolate and mix until it's evenly distributed.

8. Fill the prepared molds ⅔ full, about a rounded ¼ cup each.

9. Bake for 18 minutes. Gently rotate the pan and continue baking another 7 to 10 minutes. Bake until a tester inserted in the center comes out with moist crumbs.

10. Remove from the oven and place the pan on a wire rack set over a piece of aluminum foil. When the molds/pan are cool enough to handle, lift the molds off the cakes or flip the cakes out of the pan onto the cooling rack. Use a sharp knife to loosen the cakes around the edges if they are sticking.

11. While the cakes are still warm, dip each one in the coffee syrup, rolling it around to coat it completely, and return them to the cooling rack to dry for a few minutes.

12. Before serving, sift cocoa powder generously over each cake.

FRUIT BUCKLE

This cake disguises itself as a simple coffee cake. Its humble, homey appearance is just a modest cover for the extraordinary flavor and texture it delivers. It's a bakery favorite among staff and customers alike. We use a mixture of seasonal fruits such as plums, peaches, raspberries, and, of course, Maine-grown blueberries. Since we can't seem to survive the winter without this delectable pastry, we use frozen local blueberries to get us through till spring. *MAKES ONE 8 X 8-INCH CAKE*

For the cake batter:

1¾ CUPS PLUS 3 TABLESPOONS CAKE FLOUR

2¼ TEASPOONS BAKING POWDER

1 TEASPOON SALT

½ CUP (1 STICK) UNSALTED BUTTER, ROOM TEMPERATURE, PLUS EXTRA FOR GREASING THE PAN

1 CUP SUGAR

2 EGGS, ROOM TEMPERATURE

2 TEASPOONS VANILLA EXTRACT

1 CUP HEAVY CREAM

For the topping:

1 CUP SLICED STRAWBERRIES

1 CUP DICED RHUBARB

¼ CUP SUGAR

1½ TEASPOONS ALL-PURPOSE FLOUR

ZEST OF 1 LEMON

1 RECIPE STREUSEL (PAGE 170)

1. Position a rack in the top third of the oven and preheat the oven to 365 degrees. Lightly grease an 8 x 8-inch baking pan with butter or nonstick cooking spray.

2. To make the cake, in a medium bowl, whisk together the flour, baking powder, and salt.

3. In the bowl of a stand mixer fitted with the paddle attachment, beat the butter and sugar on medium speed until they are light and fluffy. Add the eggs, one by one, scraping down the sides of the bowl and mixing well after each addition. Add the vanilla and beat until incorporated.

4. On low speed, add one third of the flour mixture, then add half of the cream. Add the rest of the ingredients, alternating the flour with the cream.

5. Pour the mixture into the prepared baking pan and smooth the surface with an offset spatula.

6. To prepare the fruit topping, toss the strawberries, rhubarb, sugar, flour, and zest in a large bowl until the fruit is evenly coated.

7. Spread the fruit mixture over the batter. Crumble the streusel topping evenly over the fruit.

8. Bake for 30 minutes then rotate the pan from front to back. Bake an additional 20 to 25 minutes or until a cake tester comes out clean (there may be some moist fruit on the tester).

9. Remove from the oven and cool in the pan on a wire rack. The buckle can be served warm or at room temperature.

BLUEBERRY TOPPING

2 CUPS WILD BLUEBERRIES

¼ CUP SUGAR

1½ TEASPOONS ALL-PURPOSE FLOUR

ZEST OF 1 LEMON

1. Prepare the buckle batter through step 5.

2. Toss the blueberries with the sugar, flour, and zest in a large bowl until the fruit is evenly coated.

3. Follow the directions from step 7 above.

PEACH AND RASPBERRY TOPPING

1 CUP RASPBERRIES

1 CUP DICED RIPE PEACHES

¼ CUP SUGAR

1½ TEASPOONS ALL-PURPOSE FLOUR

ZEST OF 1 LEMON

1. Prepare the buckle batter through step 5.

2. Toss the raspberries and peaches with the sugar, flour, and zest in a large bowl until the fruit is evenly coated.

3. Follow the directions from step 7 above.

GINGERBREAD

We began making this cake one early fall day in our tiny bakery on Wharf Street, the earthy molasses and aromatic spices being just what we craved on a crisp New England afternoon. The following spring when we tried to remove it from our menu, there were so many requests that we continued to offer it, finding to our surprise that it was just as popular in the summer as in the winter. The thin wash of translucent lemon glaze adds a subtle bright note. *MAKES ONE 8-INCH CAKE*

2 CUPS ALL-PURPOSE FLOUR

1½ TEASPOONS BAKING SODA

2½ TEASPOONS GROUND GINGER

¼ TEASPOON GROUND CINNAMON

⅛ TEASPOON GROUND CLOVES

⅛ TEASPOON SALT

⅓ CUP (⅔ STICK) UNSALTED BUTTER, ROOM TEMPERATURE

⅓ CUP PLUS 1 TEASPOON SUGAR

1 EGG, ROOM TEMPERATURE

¾ CUP MOLASSES

¾ CUP PLUS 1 TABLESPOON COLD WATER

For the lemon glaze:

¾ CUP CONFECTIONERS' SUGAR, SIFTED

1 TABLESPOON PLUS 2 TEASPOONS FRESH LEMON JUICE

1. Position a rack in the center of the oven and preheat the oven to 375 degrees. Spray a 6-cup fluted tube pan with nonstick cooking spray.

2. In a medium bowl, whisk together the flour, baking soda, ginger, cinnamon, cloves, and salt.

3. In the bowl of a stand mixer fitted with the paddle attachment, beat the butter and sugar on medium speed until combined well. Add the egg on low speed and beat to combine. Beat in the molasses. With a rubber spatula, scrape down the paddle, the sides, and bottom of the bowl and continue beating until incorporated.

4. Add half of the flour mixture, beating until blended. Beat in the remaining flour mixture. Gradually add the cold water and beat until incorporated. Scrape down the sides of the bowl and beat until thoroughly combined.

5. Pour the batter evenly into the pan.

6. Bake 32 to 35 minutes, rotating the pan half way through the baking time. A tester inserted into the center of the cake will come out clean. Transfer to a wire rack and cool for 10 minutes. Turn the cake out of the pan onto the wire rack set over a sheet of parchment paper or aluminum foil.

7. For the lemon glaze, in a small bowl, whisk the confectioners' sugar and the lemon juice until smooth. Spoon the lemon glaze over the top of the warm cake, letting it drip randomly over the sides.

8. Serve the cake warm or at room temperature.

[

The earthy molasses and aromatic spices were just what we craved on a crisp New England afternoon.

]

MEDITERRANEAN LEMON CAKE

A celebration of Mediterranean flavors that we dream about in the heart of our lengthy Maine winter. The subtle fruitiness of olive oil complements the sweet citrus hints of lemon in this beautiful cake. Use extra virgin if you want to really showcase the olive oil flavor. This unassuming, pastoral cake becomes the highlight of a summer get-together. A generous slice on your dessert plate with a touch of fresh berries is sublime! *MAKES ONE 9-INCH CAKE*

1⅔ CUPS ALL-PURPOSE FLOUR

1½ TEASPOONS BAKING POWDER

PINCH SALT

6 TABLESPOONS (¾ STICK) UNSALTED BUTTER, MELTED AND COOLED

⅓ CUP PLUS 1 TABLESPOON OLIVE OIL

1 TABLESPOON PLUS 1 TEASPOON FRESHLY SQUEEZED LEMON JUICE

¾ CUP PLUS 2 TABLESPOONS SUGAR

ZEST FROM 2 LEMONS

4 EGGS, ROOM TEMPERATURE

2 TABLESPOONS PLUS 1½ TEASPOONS MILK, ROOM TEMPERATURE

For the lemon syrup:

¼ CUP SUGAR

JUICE FROM 1 LEMON

1. Position a rack in the top third of the oven and preheat the oven to 375 degrees. Spray a 9-inch springform pan with nonstick cooking spray.

2. In a medium bowl, whisk together the flour, baking powder, and salt.

3. In a small bowl, combine the melted butter, olive oil, and lemon juice.

4. In the bowl of a stand mixer fitted with the whisk attachment, combine the sugar and lemon zest on low speed. Add the eggs and mix on medium-high speed until the mixture is pale and airy, about 5 minutes.

5. Add the milk and mix until combined.

6. Reduce the speed to low and add the flour mixture, beating together until moistened.

7. Slowly add the butter and oil mixture, beating just until it is incorporated.

8. Pour the batter into the prepared pan and bake for 30 minutes, rotating the pan half way through the baking time. The cake should spring back when gently pressed in the center. Remove from the oven and place it on a cooling rack for about 10 minutes.

9. Make the lemon syrup by placing the sugar, ¼ cup water, and lemon juice in a small pan. Heat the mixture to a boil, stirring occasionally to ensure that the sugar is dissolved. Remove from the heat and cover to keep warm.

10. After the cake has cooled slightly, run a knife between the side of the cake and the pan and remove the springform ring. Place a piece of parchment paper or aluminum foil underneath the cooling rack and place the cake on the rack.

11. Gently drizzle and brush the warm lemon syrup over the entire top and sides of the warm cake using a pastry brush.

PUMPKIN BRIOCHE BREAD PUDDING

During the fall and winter holidays we bake dozens of these warm, spiced puddings in successive batches. It can be served warm from the oven with cream, at room temperature, or slightly chilled. Croissants or challah could also be used in place of the brioche, or for just a portion of it.

MAKES ONE 9X9-INCH BREAD PUDDING

1 CUP RAISINS

¼ CUP RUM

¼ CUP HOT WATER

8 CUPS CUBED BRIOCHE, PREFERABLY DAY OLD, LIGHTLY PACKED

4 EGGS

1 CUP SUGAR

1⅓ CUPS WHOLE MILK

2 TEASPOONS VANILLA EXTRACT

1 TEASPOON GROUND CINNAMON

1 TEASPOON GROUND GINGER

⅛ TEASPOON GROUND ALLSPICE

PINCH SALT

1½ CUPS PUMPKIN PUREE

CONFECTIONERS' SUGAR, FOR DUSTING

1. Butter a 9-x-9-inch baking pan.

2. Position a rack in the middle of the oven. Preheat the oven to 325 degrees.

3. Place the raisins in a small bowl and cover with the rum and hot water. Let them soak until plump, about 20 minutes. Drain and set aside.

4. Spread the cubed bread on a baking sheet. Bake at 325 degrees for 5 to 10 minutes or until lightly toasted. Remove from the oven and let cool.

5. In a large bowl, whisk together the eggs, sugar, milk, vanilla, cinnamon, ginger, allspice, and salt. Add the pumpkin puree and stir until smooth and well combined. Toss in the toasted bread cubes and stir gently until the bread is evenly coated.

6. Let the pudding mixture sit for about 15 minutes. Gently stir the mixture a few times while it's sitting. It's ready when the bread is well moistened and most of the liquid has been absorbed.

7. Fold in the drained raisins, then scrape the mixture into the prepared baking pan. Place the baking pan in a roasting pan. Pour hot water into the roasting pan until it reaches halfway up the sides of the pudding pan.

8. Carefully transfer to the oven and bake until the custard has set in the center and the top is golden, about 55 to 60 minutes. The center should feel firm and the surface will be dry to the touch. A cake-tester inserted into the center will come out clean. If it's browning too quickly, cover the top loosely with aluminum foil.

9. Remove from the oven and transfer the bread pudding pan to a wire rack to cool for about 20 minutes before serving. The pudding can be served as is or dusted with confectioners' sugar just before serving.

PECAN FINANCIER

The financier is a classic French pastry found in boulangeries and patisseries all over France. Typically made from ground almonds and baked in shallow rectangular molds, they resemble gold bars, hence the name. Ellen Donati Lyford, one of our talented pastry and bread bakers, developed this somewhat more decadent recipe, built on toasted pecans embellished with dark bittersweet chocolate. Our good friend and longtime bakery customer, Helio Medina, who was born in Portugal and is a master home cook, once served us a vintage port to pair with these. The combination was magical. A.P.

Note: This recipe requires some refrigeration time, so plan accordingly. To minimize the waiting time, you could mix it the day before you plan to do your baking and refrigerate the batter overnight. In any case, the batter should be chilled when it goes into the oven. We use small brioche molds, but a muffin tin would work just as well. *MAKES 14 TO 16 SMALL CAKES*

½ CUP (1 STICK) UNSALTED BUTTER

2½ CUPS TOASTED PECANS (SEE INSTRUCTIONS ON PAGE 170)

2 CUPS SUGAR

⅔ CUP ALL-PURPOSE FLOUR

¾ TEASPOON SALT

1 CUP (ABOUT 7 EGGS) EGG WHITES, ROOM TEMPERATURE

¾ CUP BITTERSWEET CHOCOLATE CHUNKS

1. To brown the butter, place it in a small saucepan, melt it over medium heat, and simmer gently. Remove it from the heat when the milk solids on the bottom begin to brown and give off a nutty aroma. Set aside and let it cool to room temperature.

2. Place the pecans in the bowl of a food processor and pulse on and off until they are reduced to very small pieces —but not into a flour or paste consistency.

3. In a large bowl, mix the sugar, nuts, flour, and salt together.

4. Whisk the egg whites into the dry mixture, then add the cooled butter, making sure to scrape all the browned butter solids into the mixture. Mix until thoroughly combined.

5. Refrigerate the batter for 1 to 2 hours or overnight. If you are baking on the same day, position a rack in the center of the oven and preheat the oven to 375 degrees about half an hour before you fill the molds.

6. Spray the brioche molds or muffin tin cups generously with nonstick cooking spray.

7. Fill the molds or cups with the batter, leaving ½ inch at the top. Refrigerate any unused batter.

8. Place several chocolate chunks in the center of each mold, each one resting on top of the batter.

9. Place the molds on a baking sheet, evenly spaced. If using a muffin tin, place it directly on the oven rack.

10. Bake for 25 minutes, rotating the pan half way through the baking time. The centers should be set and the edges dark brown. Remove from the oven and place on a wire rack. Before the financiers are completely cool, use a butter knife or small spatula to flip them out of the cups, or turn the pan upside down and tap lightly to release them. They can be eaten warm, but they really are better after a few hours when the batter has set, the centers are still moist and buttery, and the exterior is crisp and chewy.

11. When the pan or brioche molds have cooled, lightly re-spray with nonstick cooking spray. Remove the remaining batter from the refrigerator and bake as indicated above.

SUMMER BERRY BUTTERMILK CAKE

A rustic-looking cake we could imagine on the table of every Italian grandmother. We like how the tangy buttermilk and tart berries hold the sweetness in balance. The flavor and texture seems to improve each day, as a friend noted, when he told us that it reminded him of his favorite cheesecake. *MAKES ONE 9-INCH CAKE*

1¼ CUPS ALL-PURPOSE FLOUR

¼ CUP SEMOLINA FLOUR

1½ TEASPOONS BAKING POWDER

½ TEASPOON SALT

6 TABLESPOONS UNSALTED BUTTER, SOFTENED, PLUS EXTRA FOR GREASING PAN

1 CUP LOOSELY PACKED DARK BROWN SUGAR

1 LARGE EGG, ROOM TEMPERATURE

½ CUP BUTTERMILK, ROOM TEMPERATURE

1 TEASPOON VANILLA EXTRACT

6 TO 8 OUNCES FRESH BLACKBERRIES, HALVED IF LARGE, OR RASPBERRIES

2 TABLESPOONS TURBINADO SUGAR, FOR DUSTING

CONFECTIONERS' SUGAR, FOR GARNISH (OPTIONAL)

1. Position a rack in the center of the oven and preheat the oven to 350 degrees. Butter a 9-inch cake pan. Line the bottom of the pan with a circle of parchment paper, then butter the paper as well.

2. In a large bowl, whisk together the all-purpose flour, semolina flour, baking powder, and salt.

3. In the bowl of a stand mixer fitted with the paddle attachment, beat the butter and brown sugar on medium speed until light and fluffy, about 3 minutes.

4. Reduce the speed to low and add the egg, buttermilk, and vanilla. Gradually add in the flour mixture, scraping down the sides of the bowl and paddle as needed. Beat until just incorporated.

5. Scrape the batter into the prepared pan. Arrange the berries close together on top of the batter. Sprinkle the turbinado sugar over the berries.

6. Bake for 10 minutes and then reduce the oven temperature to 325 degrees. Bake for another 20 minutes. Gently rotate the pan in the oven and continue baking until the center is firm to the touch, 15 to 20 minutes longer.

7. Remove from the oven and place on a wire rack to cool for about 20 minutes. Run the thin edge of a table knife between the pan and the outer edge of the cake to loosen the sides. Place the wire rack on top of the pan, invert the cake onto the rack, and gently lift the pan to remove. If the parchment paper is stuck to the cake, gently remove it. Cover with a plate, invert the cake right side up, and remove the rack. Allow to cool completely. Dust lightly with confectioners' sugar before serving.

[
A rustic-looking cake we could imagine on the table of every Italian grandmother.
]

TRIPLE CHOCOLATE CAKE

We have all had cakes that promised actual chocolate flavor but didn't deliver. This recipe is the answer to all of your chocolate cake hopes and expectations. It is incredibly rich and moist, loaded with shards of bittersweet chocolate, and topped with a smooth, creamy ganache. It is essential to use a high-quality chocolate, one that you enjoy eating on its own. *MAKES ONE 8-INCH CAKE*

For the cake:
⅓ CUP DUTCH-PROCESSED COCOA POWDER
¼ CUP HOT WATER
3 EGGS
1½ TEASPOONS VANILLA EXTRACT
¾ CUP PLUS 2 TABLESPOONS ALL-PURPOSE FLOUR
1 CUP SUGAR
1 TEASPOON BAKING POWDER
PINCH SALT
⅔ CUP (1⅓ STICK) UNSALTED BUTTER, ROOM TEMPERATURE
2 CUPS (10 OUNCES) CHOPPED BITTERSWEET CHOCOLATE

For the coffee syrup:
½ CUP STRONG BREWED COFFEE
2 TEASPOONS SUGAR

For the ganache:
¾ CUP (ABOUT 4 OUNCES) CHOPPED BITTERSWEET CHOCOLATE
¼ CUP HALF-AND-HALF

1. In a medium bowl or a glass measuring cup, stir together the sugar and the hot coffee. Set the syrup aside to cool.

2. Position a rack in the top third of the oven and preheat the oven to 350 degrees. Spray a 6-cup fluted tube pan with nonstick cooking spray.

3. In a medium bowl, stir together the hot water and cocoa powder to make a stiff paste. Add the eggs and vanilla and stir until combined (the mixture will be very lumpy).

4. In a medium bowl, whisk together the flour, sugar, baking powder, and salt.

5. In the bowl of a stand mixer fitted with the paddle attachment, beat the butter on medium speed until it's smooth. Add the flour mixture and beat on medium speed until incorporated. Add the cocoa mixture and mix on low until the dry ingredients are evenly moistened.

6. Beat on medium speed for an additional minute to aerate the mixture. It should become the color of milk chocolate.

7. Reduce the speed to low, add the chopped chocolate, and mix until it's evenly distributed.

8. Pour the mixture into the prepared pan. Bake for 20 minutes. Gently rotate the pan in the oven and continue baking another 20 to 23 minutes, until a tester inserted in the center comes out with moist crumbs.

9. Remove the cake from the oven and place the pan on a wire rack to cool slightly. When the pan is cool enough to handle but still warm, set a piece of parchment paper underneath the rack and turn the cake out of the pan onto the rack.

10. While the cake is still warm, brush the coffee syrup over the entire surface with a pastry brush. Continue cooling the cake to room temperature.

11. Make the ganache. Place the chopped chocolate in a small heat-proof bowl. In a small pan, heat the half-and-half to nearly a boil and pour it over the chocolate. Let the mixture stand for a minute and then stir it gently with a rubber spatula until it's smooth.

12. Pour the warm ganache over the top of the cake, allowing it to run down the sides. Let it sit at room temperature for 10 to 15 minutes before serving in order for the ganache to set.

> *The cake is incredibly rich and moist, loaded with shards of bittersweet chocolate.*

VANILLA BEAN SHORTCAKES

There are so many different types of shortcakes. Ours are tender, moist, loaded with vanilla, and a touch of buttermilk gives them the perfect amount of tanginess. The sweetness comes primarily from the sparkly crystals of sugar sprinkled on top—and, of course, from the ripe berries you layer into them! *MAKES 12 SHORTCAKES*

⅔ CUP BUTTERMILK

⅓ CUP HALF-AND-HALF

1 EGG

1 TABLESPOON PLUS 2 TEASPOONS VANILLA EXTRACT

1 VANILLA BEAN

3¼ CUPS ALL-PURPOSE FLOUR

¼ CUP PLUS 1 TABLESPOON PACKED DARK BROWN SUGAR

1 TEASPOON SALT

1 TABLESPOON PLUS 1¼ TEASPOONS BAKING POWDER

10 TABLESPOONS UNSALTED BUTTER, CUT INTO ½-INCH CUBES, CHILLED

¼ CUP COARSE WHITE COOKIE DECORATING SUGAR

1. Position a rack in the center of the oven and preheat the oven to 375 degrees. Line a baking sheet with parchment paper.

2. In a small bowl, whisk together the buttermilk, half-and-half, egg, and vanilla extract. With the tip of a sharp knife, split the vanilla bean lengthwise. Scrape the seeds into the egg mixture and stir together.

3. In a large bowl, whisk together the flour, brown sugar, salt, and baking powder.

4. Add the cubed butter and work it into the flour mixture with your fingertips until a few pea-size chunks of butter remain.

5. Add the egg mixture to the flour mixture and combine them using a fork or your hands until the dry ingredients are fully moistened.

6. Using an ice cream scoop or a ¼-cup measure, gently fill the scoop and drop the mounds, evenly spaced, onto the baking sheet. Sprinkle each one lightly with decorating sugar.

7. Bake for 22 to 24 minutes, rotating the baking sheet after 12 minutes for even baking. They will have golden spots and feel firm in the center.

8. Remove from the oven and transfer the shortcakes to a wire rack to cool slightly. These are best when served still warm from the oven, with local berries and freshly whipped cream.

VANILLA BEAN MADELEINES

In Marcel Proust's, *In Search of Lost Time* (aka *Remembrance of Things Past*), an experience of "involuntary memory" involving a madeleine cookie causes the narrator to experience childhood time spent in the village of Combray in a flood of memories. The enjoyment of food is often intertwined with memories of family, friends, and events. We can't help but think how many new madeleine-inspired memories we've helped create. These vanilla and honey cakes are eaten by the hundreds by countless vacationers and locals—a future madeleine may have them reminiscing about a little bakery on the coast of Maine... *MAKES 12 MADELEINES*

4 TABLESPOONS UNSALTED BUTTER

½ VANILLA BEAN

½ CUP SIFTED CONFECTIONERS' SUGAR

2 TEASPOONS PACKED DARK BROWN SUGAR

2½ TEASPOONS HONEY

2 EGGS, ROOM TEMPERATURE

½ TEASPOON VANILLA EXTRACT

½ CUP PLUS 2 TABLESPOONS ALL-PURPOSE FLOUR

½ TEASPOON BAKING POWDER

PINCH SALT

1. Position a rack in the center of the oven and preheat the oven to 375 degrees. Spray a 12-piece madeleine mold with nonstick cooking spray and set it on a baking sheet.

2. In a small saucepan, melt the butter. Slice the vanilla bean lengthwise and scrape the seeds into the hot butter. Transfer the butter into the bowl of a stand mixer fitted with the paddle attachment. Add the confectioners' sugar and beat on low speed until smooth.

4. Add the brown sugar and the honey, then add the eggs one at a time, mixing on low speed. Scrape down the sides of the bowl as needed. Add the vanilla extract and beat until combined.

5. In a small bowl, whisk together the flour, baking powder, and salt. Add the flour mixture to the mixer and beat until just combined, being careful not to over mix.

6. Portion the batter into the prepared madeleine pan. Fill the molds ⅔ full, about a heaping tablespoon each. Bake for 12 minutes, rotating the pan after about 6 minutes to ensure even baking. They should feel just firm in the center and be lightly browned on the edges.

7. Remove from the oven and transfer to a wire rack, letting the madeleines cool for 10 minutes before removing from the pan. Madeleines can be eaten warm or at room temperature.

COOKIES

Is there anything more comforting than the aroma of cookies baking? Everyone has fond memories of childhood favorites—Toll House, oatmeal, peanut butter, and sugar cookies. Nothing is more satisfying than devouring two or three, warm from the oven, with a glass of cold milk.

At Standard Baking Co., many customers visit us every afternoon like clockwork for their daily cookie fix. In the summer months, day-trippers heading off to the beach often stop here first to load up on Molasses Cookies or Chocolate Sablés. In the fall and winter we add more elaborate holiday items to our menu, like the Linzer and Hazelnut Sandwich Cookies. But you can bake and enjoy your favorites any time of year.

At the bakery, multiple steps must be perfectly coordinated so that fresh-from-the-oven cookies appear on our pastry counter throughout the day—like those well-stocked cookie jars of childhood.

As a home baker, there are just a few things you need to keep in mind. Be sure to start with room temperature ingredients, and always use a room temperature baking sheet, unless otherwise specified in a recipe. You don't want to take any shortcuts—no matter how excited you are to eat your cookies. All of these recipes tell you how many cookies bake well on a sheet, and whether you can bake more than one sheet at a time. If you can curb your enthusiasm to bake them quickly, the results will be well worth it.

ALMOND BISCOTTI

Also known as cantuccini or biscotti di Prato, this recipe is a Tuscan tradition. Made without added fat, its crisp, almost hard texture is a perfect accompaniment to coffee or the customary sweet Tuscan wine, Vin Santo. For a more refined variation, we like to slice these very thinly, about ¼-inch thick. *MAKES 48 BISCOTTI*

3½ CUPS ALL-PURPOSE FLOUR

1 TABLESPOON BAKING POWDER

1¼ TEASPOONS GROUND CINNAMON

½ TEASPOON SALT

1¼ CUPS SUGAR

4 EGGS PLUS 1 EGG YOLK

1 TABLESPOON VANILLA EXTRACT

2¾ CUPS WHOLE ALMONDS, TOASTED (SEE INSTRUCTIONS ON PAGE 170)

1. Position a rack in the center of the oven and preheat the oven to 350 degrees. Line a baking sheet with parchment paper.

2. In the bowl of a standing mixer fitted with the paddle attachment, combine the flour, baking powder, cinnamon, salt, and sugar on medium speed.

3. In a small bowl, combine the eggs and the vanilla.

4. Add the egg mixture to the flour mixture and beat until a cohesive dough is formed.

5. Add the almonds on low speed and mix until well distributed. You may need to stop the mixer and push the almonds in by hand every so often.

6. Transfer the dough to a work surface and divide it into two equal pieces. Roughly shape each piece into a 14-inch-long log. Transfer each log to the baking sheet, leaving about 3 inches between them. Wet your fingers and flatten each log until it's about 2 ½ inches wide and ¾ inch thick.

7. Bake the logs for 32 to 35 minutes, rotating the baking sheet half way through the baking time. The logs should be slightly risen and firm to the touch. Remove from the oven and cool completely on a wire rack.

8. Reduce the oven temperature to 325 degrees. Transfer the logs to a cutting surface and, using a sharp knife, cut on the diagonal into ½-inch-wide slices. Place the slices side by side, cut side down, on a baking sheet lined with parchment paper. Bake for 20 minutes, rotating the baking sheet half way through the baking time. The biscotti are done when they are very crisp.

9. Remove from the oven, cool completely on a wire rack.

ALMOND MACAROONS

Moist and chewy, these tiny two-bite morsels are more of a confection than a cookie. We initially baked these for Passover because they are made without wheat or any of the other grains that are avoided in observance of the holiday. We received so many requests that we now bake them at least twice weekly, all year round. *MAKES ABOUT 20 COOKIES*

2½ CUPS SLICED ALMONDS
¾ CUP SUGAR
¼ TEASPOON SALT
1 TEASPOON LEMON JUICE
⅓ CUP EGG WHITES (2 EGGS), CHILLED
SLIVERED ALMONDS, AS GARNISH (OPTIONAL)

1. Position a rack in the middle of the oven and preheat the oven to 375 degrees. Line a baking sheet with parchment paper.

2. In a food processor fitted with the blade attachment, process the almonds and sugar together until they are coarsely ground. Add the salt and process for 2 to 3 seconds more.

3. Transfer the almond mixture to a large bowl and stir in the egg whites and lemon juice using a rubber spatula. Stir until all the dry ingredients are moistened. The mixture will form a ball and clean the sides of the bowl.

4. Drop lightly packed, heaping tablespoonfuls of the mixture onto the baking sheet, evenly spaced about 2 inches apart. Place 2 to 3 slivered almonds on each mound, if using.

5. Bake for 14 to 15 minutes, rotating the baking sheet half way through the baking time. The macaroons will be lightly browned on the edges and firm to the touch.

6. Transfer to a wire rack to cool completely. Store in an airtight container.

BACI

Pronounced *BAH-chee*, which means "kisses" in Italian, we make hundreds of these fine-textured shortbread sandwich cookies every Valentine's Day. This recipe was contributed by one of our former pastry chefs, Jackie King, who has since opened a successful bakery in Massachusetts, called A & J King Artisan Bakers, with her husband Andy, a bread baker. We think the quantity of ganache in this recipe is just the right amount —but if you are a "frosting taster," you may want to double it! *MAKES 24 COOKIES*

For the chocolate ganache:
½ CUP, HEAPING (2.5 OUNCES), FINELY CHOPPED BITTERSWEET CHOCOLATE
⅛ CUP HALF-AND-HALF

For the cookies:
1½ CUPS PLUS 1 TABLESPOON ALL-PURPOSE FLOUR
¼ TEASPOON SALT
¾ CUP PLUS 1 TABLESPOON (1⅔ STICKS) UNSALTED BUTTER, ROOM TEMPERATURE
½ CUP CONFECTIONERS' SUGAR, SIFTED
1 TABLESPOON RUM

1. To make the ganache, place the chopped chocolate in a small heat-proof bowl. In a small pan, heat the half-and-half to nearly a boil and pour it over the chocolate. Let the mixture stand for a minute and then stir it gently with a rubber spatula until smooth. Set it aside to cool. The ganache needs to be cooled to a paste consistency before filling the cookies or the halves will slide off each other.

2. To make the cookie dough, whisk together the flour and salt in a medium bowl and set aside.

3. In the bowl of a stand mixer fitted with a paddle attachment, combine the butter and confectioners' sugar and beat on medium speed until incorporated. Add the rum and beat a few seconds more. Stop the mixer and, using a plastic scraper or rubber spatula, scrape down the sides of the bowl.

4. On low speed, slowly add the flour and salt and beat until incorporated. Scrape down the sides of the bowl and paddle. Cover the bowl and place it in the refrigerator for about 1 hour before shaping the cookies. This step helps make the cookies easier to form.

5. When the dough is chilled and firm, remove it from the refrigerator. Form the dough into twenty-four 1-inch balls. Place the balls on a plate and freeze for 20 minutes, until very firm.

6. While dough is in the freezer, position the racks in the top and bottom thirds of the oven and preheat the oven to 375 degrees. Line two baking sheets with parchment paper.

7. When the dough is very firm, remove it from the freezer. Carefully cut each ball in half and place the cut sides down on the baking sheets, evenly spaced. Bake twenty-four cookies per sheet.

8. Bake for 8 minutes, then rotate the baking sheets front to back and top to bottom. Bake an additional 6 minutes or until they are just starting to become golden brown at the bottom edges. Remove from the oven and place on a wire rack to cool.

9. Once cooled, the cookies can be filled with the room-temperature ganache. Using a knife or an offset spatula, spread about ¾ teaspoon of ganache on the bottom of a cookie. Place the bottom of another cookie on the chocolate to form a sandwich, and repeat in the same manner with the rest of the cookies.

BISCOTTI DI POLENTA

These crunchy, lemony cookies have a surprise kick of black pepper. We find that customers can be a little timid about trying them, but when we put out samples they are gone in seconds! We love the flavor and texture that yellow cornmeal brings to baked goods, especially these. Luckily, corn is a traditional New England crop so we have access to locally-grown, freshly milled, organic yellow cornmeal. Coarsely ground cornmeal is used in this recipe but feel free to experiment with substitutes, such as white cornmeal or a finer grind. Just be sure to use fresh cornmeal. As with any whole grains, the oil in the grain will turn rancid over time. *MAKES ABOUT 36 COOKIES*

1 CUP ALL-PURPOSE FLOUR
¾ CUP STONE-GROUND CORNMEAL
½ TEASPOON FRESHLY GROUND BLACK PEPPER
PINCH SALT
¾ CUP (1½ STICKS) UNSALTED BUTTER, ROOM TEMPERATURE
¾ CUP SUGAR
⅛ CUP FINELY GRATED LEMON ZEST (FROM 2 LEMONS)
1 EGG YOLK, ROOM TEMPERATURE

1. In a medium bowl, combine the flour, cornmeal, pepper, and salt.

2. In the bowl of a stand mixer fitted with the paddle attachment, beat the butter, sugar, and zest starting on low speed. Increase to medium-high speed until light and fluffy.

3. On low speed, add the egg yolk, and mix until combined.

4. Add the flour mixture, and mix on low speed, stopping the mixer to scrape down the bowl and the paddle frequently. Mix until incorporated.

5. On a lightly floured surface or silicone mat, roll the cookie dough into a 12-inch-long log. Flatten the log into a rough rectangular shape, 12 inches x 2 inches by 1 inch.

6. Wrap the log in plastic wrap and chill in the refrigerator until firm, 45 minutes to 1 hour.

7. Position the racks in the top and bottom thirds of the oven and preheat the oven to 400 degrees. Line two baking sheets with parchment paper.

8. Cut the log into slices ¼ inch thick and place on the baking sheet equally spaced.

9. Bake for 8 minutes, then rotate the baking sheets front to back and top to bottom. Bake an additional 6 minutes or until the edges of the cookies are deep golden brown. Transfer to a wire rack to cool.

BUTTER COOKIES

Thin, crisp, and buttery, this delicate dough can be cut into any shape imaginable. Its convenience is unsurpassed, as you can mix it days or weeks ahead of time, then roll it out, and bake it at the last minute. Just give the dough a few minutes after removing it from the refrigerator before rolling, and it will be smooth and pliable. This recipe calls for a 2¼ round cookie cutter, if you use a different size, you may need to adjust the baking time. *MAKES 80 COOKIES*

3 CUPS ALL-PURPOSE FLOUR
¼ TEASPOON SALT
¾ CUP PLUS 2 TABLESPOONS (1¾ STICKS) UNSALTED BUTTER, ROOM TEMPERATURE
¾ CUP SUGAR
¾ TEASPOON VANILLA EXTRACT
2 EGGS, ROOM TEMPERATURE

1. In a medium bowl, whisk together the flour and salt.

2. In the bowl of a stand mixer fitted with the paddle attachment, beat the butter on medium speed for 1 to 2 minutes, or until smooth and creamy.

3. Add the sugar and continue beating on medium speed until incorporated.

4. On low speed, add the vanilla, then add the eggs one at a time and beat between additions. Scrape down the sides of the bowl and beat until incorporated.

5. On low speed, gradually add the flour mixture, stopping the mixer occasionally to scrape down the sides of the bowl and the paddle. Continue mixing until all ingredients are incorporated, being careful not to over mix.

6. Transfer the dough to a work surface and divide it into four or five equal pieces. Flatten each piece into a disc and wrap each one in plastic wrap. Refrigerate for up to five days or freeze for up to a month. (Frozen dough should be defrosted before proceeding.)

7. When you're ready to roll out the dough, position the racks in the top and bottom thirds of the oven and preheat the oven to 375 degrees. Line two baking sheets with parchment paper.

8. Working with one disc at a time, remove it from the refrigerator, unwrap, and place it on a lightly floured work surface or silicone mat. With a rolling pin, roll the disc into a sheet about ⅛ inch thick. If the dough becomes too soft and sticky while you're working, just return it to the refrigerator for a few minutes to firm up.

9. Using a 2¼-inch round cookie cutter, cut out as many pieces as possible and place them on the prepared baking sheets, evenly spaced, and at least ½ inch apart. Reserve the scraps off to the side of your work surface and, when you've finished cutting out all the cookies, gently mold the scraps together into a disc shape. Wrap it with plastic wrap and refrigerate it until chilled. Follow the directions from the beginning of Step 8.

10. Bake for 5 minutes, then rotate the baking sheets from front to back and top to bottom. Bake an additional 5 minutes, or until the centers feel firm and the edges are lightly browned.

11. Remove from the oven and transfer to a wire rack until completely cooled.

> *Thin, crisp, and buttery, this delicate dough can be cut into any shape imaginable.*

CHOCOLATE CHIP COOKIES

The best thing about baking larger cookies, besides the fact that you get more bites, is that it is easier to achieve a contrast in textures. We bake ours to a deep brown hue, until the edges are crisp and well caramelized, while the centers remain moist and slightly cake-like. It's best to cool them directly on a cooling rack so that the bottoms do not become soggy. *MAKES 12 COOKIES*

2¾ CUPS ALL-PURPOSE FLOUR

1 TEASPOON SALT

1 TEASPOON BAKING SODA

1¼ CUP (2½ STICKS) UNSALTED BUTTER, ROOM TEMPERATURE

¾ CUP PLUS 1 TABLESPOON GRANULATED SUGAR

¾ CUP PACKED DARK BROWN SUGAR

2 EGGS, ROOM TEMPERATURE

1 TEASPOON VANILLA EXTRACT

2 CUPS BITTERSWEET CHOCOLATE CHUNKS

1. Position the oven racks in the top and bottom thirds of the oven and preheat the oven to 375 degrees. Line two baking sheets with parchment paper.

2. In a large bowl, whisk together the flour, salt, and baking soda.

3. In the bowl of a stand mixer fitted with the paddle attachment, beat the butter on medium speed until smooth and creamy.

4. Add the granulated and brown sugars and beat on medium speed until light and fluffy, stopping the mixer to scrape down the bowl and paddle frequently.

5. Add the eggs and vanilla on low speed and mix until just combined, scraping down the bowl and paddle as needed.

6. On low speed, add the flour mixture in ⅓ increments, mixing gently and scraping down the bowl as needed until thoroughly blended.

7. Slowly add in the chocolate chunks and mix gently until they are evenly distributed.

8. Using an ice cream scoop, or forming into 2-inch balls, drop mounds of the dough onto the baking sheets, evenly spaced, six per tray.

9. Bake for 8 minutes, rotate the baking sheets from front to back and top to bottom, and bake 8 minutes more. The cookies will spread slightly but remain thicker in the center and have dark brown edges.

10. Remove from the oven and transfer the cookies onto a wire rack. The centers will sink slightly and the edges should be crisp and deeply caramelized.

OATMEAL RAISIN COOKIES

While most oatmeal cookie recipes are spiced with cinnamon, ours are lightly laced with freshly ground nutmeg. This cookie contains just a sprinkle of this fragrant, sweet spice —just enough to add a touch of goodness without overpowering the delicate oats and the jammy raisins. These generous cookies are crisp on the outside and chewy on the inside. *MAKES 16 COOKIES*

1½ CUPS ALL-PURPOSE FLOUR

½ TEASPOON SALT

1 TEASPOON BAKING POWDER

¼ TEASPOON FRESHLY GRATED NUTMEG

¾ CUP PLUS 2 TABLESPOONS (1¾ STICKS) UNSALTED BUTTER, ROOM TEMPERATURE

¾ CUP PLUS 3 TABLESPOONS GRANULATED SUGAR

¾ CUP PLUS 3 TABLESPOONS PACKED DARK BROWN SUGAR

2 EGGS, ROOM TEMPERATURE

2½ CUPS ROLLED OATS

1¼ CUPS RAISINS

1. Position racks in the top and bottom thirds of the oven and preheat the oven to 375 degrees. Line two baking sheets with parchment paper.

2. In a medium bowl, whisk the flour, salt, baking powder, and nutmeg together.

3. In the bowl of a stand mixer fitted with the paddle attachment, beat the butter until smooth and creamy. Add the granulated sugar and brown sugar and beat on medium speed until light and fluffy.

4. On low speed, add the eggs one at a time, beating between additions.

5. Slowly add the flour mixture into the butter mixture. Beat until thoroughly combined, scraping down the sides of the bowl and paddle as needed.

6. Gradually add the oats and raisins and mix until evenly distributed.

7. Using an ice cream scoop, or forming into 2-inch balls with your hands, drop mounds of the dough onto the baking sheets, evenly spaced six per tray. Scoop all of the dough and set the remaining pieces aside until the baking sheets have cooled after baking.

8. Bake for 10 minutes, rotate the baking sheets from front to back and top to bottom, and bake for 10 to 12 minutes longer. The edges of the cookies should be golden brown and the centers should be puffy and feel set when touched lightly. They might seem slightly under-baked, but they get crisper as they cool.

9. Remove from the oven and cool completely on a wire rack. Bake the remaining dough after the baking sheets have cooled, as directed from step 8 above.

CHOCOLATE WALNUT BISCOTTI

We adapted this recipe from one found in the late *Gourmet* magazine, about twenty years ago. These are rich and more cake-like than traditional Italian biscotti because of the high quantity of butter. We like to use a dark Belgian cocoa powder, which gives these biscotti their deep, almost black color and rich flavor. The walnuts should be toasted first to sharpen their flavor. You can use any chocolate that you like, but we prefer bittersweet chunks to balance the sweetness of the dough. So there's no waste, the scrap ends of the logs can be crumbled and used as an ice cream topping. *MAKES 32 BISCOTTI*

3 CUPS ALL-PURPOSE FLOUR

¾ CUP PLUS 1 TABLESPOON DUTCH-PROCESSED COCOA POWDER

2 TEASPOONS BAKING SODA

1½ TEASPOONS SALT

½ CUP (1 STICK) UNSALTED BUTTER, ROOM TEMPERATURE

1½ CUPS SUGAR

3 EGGS, ROOM TEMPERATURE

1 CUP WALNUT HALVES, TOASTED (SEE INSTRUCTIONS ON PAGE 170)

1¼ CUPS BITTERSWEET CHOCOLATE CHUNKS

For the egg wash:

1 EGG

PINCH SALT

1. Position a rack in the center of the oven and preheat the oven to 375 degrees. Line a baking sheet with parchment paper.

2. In a medium bowl, whisk together the flour, cocoa, baking soda, and salt.

3. In the bowl of a stand mixer fitted with the paddle attachment, cream the butter and sugar until light and fluffy.

4. On low speed, add the eggs one at a time to the butter mixture, stopping the mixer occasionally to scrape down the sides of the bowl and the paddle. Beat on low speed until thoroughly combined.

5. Gradually add the flour mixture while beating on low speed. Beat the batter until all ingredients are thoroughly incorporated, stopping the mixer occasionally to scrape down the sides of the bowl.

6. On low speed, mix in the walnuts and the chocolate chunks until they are evenly distributed.

7. Divide the dough into two equal pieces. On a lightly floured work surface or silicone mat, roll each piece into a log about 12 inches long. Place the logs lengthwise, about 3 inches apart, on the baking sheet. Press each log down with the palm of your hand to flatten the tops slightly and lengthen them to about 14 inches x 3 inches x ½-inch thick.

8. In a small bowl, make the egg wash, beating the egg, 1 teaspoon of water, and salt with a fork. With a pastry brush, lightly brush the tops and sides of the logs with the egg wash.

9. Bake for 19 to 20 minutes, rotating the baking sheet half way through the baking time. The logs will crack lengthwise and double in width. The center of each log should be firm to the touch.

10. Remove from the oven and let the logs cool on a wire rack. Reduce the oven temperature to 325 degrees. Once the logs have cooled completely, place them on a cutting board and slice them on the diagonal into ¾-inch-thick slices. A sharp knife will be helpful as the logs tend to be crumbly.

11. Place the slices side by side, cut-side down on a parchment-lined baking sheet and bake for 24 minutes, rotating the tray half way through the baking time. The biscotti are done when they are very crisp. Check the tips and edges carefully to avoid burning.

12. Remove from the oven and transfer to a wire rack to cool completely.

> # *We like to use a dark Belgian cocoa powder, which gives these biscotti their deep, almost black color and rich flavor.*

COCONUT MACAROONS

A good friend challenged me to make the perfect coconut macaroon. I tried every recipe I could find, all without success. Years later I stumbled upon the technique of cooking the macaroon mixture in a pot before baking it. The secret was discovered! These macaroons have the most amazing texture, toasty and crisp on the outside, chewy yet delicate on the inside. T.S.

Note: Look for this coconut in the natural food section of your grocery store, specialty foods store, or online. It is sometimes called "macaroon coconut." It is very finely shredded, dehydrated, and unsweetened. *MAKES 40 TO 42 MACAROONS*

4¾ CUPS UNSWEETENED FINELY SHREDDED COCONUT
1¾ CUPS SUGAR
¾ CUP (6 EGGS) EGG WHITES
½ TEASPOON SALT
1 TEASPOON VANILLA EXTRACT

1. Position two oven racks in the upper and lower thirds of the oven and preheat the oven to 375 degrees. Line two baking sheets with parchment paper.

2. In a medium saucepan, combine all the ingredients and cook, stirring continuously, on medium-low heat until a temperature of 130 degrees is reached on a candy thermometer. The mixture will seem very dry at first, but it will moisten as it cooks. It will become sticky and have a texture like mashed potatoes. Remove the pan from the heat and let it cool slightly.

3. Scoop the batter into rounded tablespoons and drop them onto the prepared baking sheet, evenly spaced. Wet your fingers to prevent sticking, then use your thumb and first two fingers to form each mound into a pyramid shape.

4. Bake for 5 minutes, then rotate baking sheets front to back and top to bottom. Bake an additional 5 to 6 minutes until the edges are browned.

5. Remove from the oven and cool completely on a wire rack.

HAMANTASCHEN

Hamantaschen are a traditional Jewish pastry. They are most often found during Purim, however, many of its biggest fans don't realize it is associated with a specific holiday, and are excited to find them appearing on the menu. A small circle of buttery dough is folded up into a triangle around a deeply sweet and tangy fruit filling. These unique little cookies are so popular that we make tray after tray of them every spring. *MAKES 45 HAMANTASCHEN*

2¼ CUPS PLUS 1 TABLESPOON ALL-PURPOSE FLOUR

2 TABLESPOONS BAKING POWDER

½ TEASPOON SALT

½ CUP (1 STICK) UNSALTED BUTTER, ROOM TEMPERATURE

1⅛ CUPS SUGAR

1 EGG, ROOM TEMPERATURE

2 TABLESPOONS ORANGE JUICE

¼ TEASPOON VANILLA EXTRACT

1 RECIPE FIG, CHERRY, OR APRICOT FILLING (RECIPES FOLLOW)

1. In a medium bowl, whisk together the flour, baking powder, and salt.

2. In the bowl of a stand mixer fitted with the paddle attachment, beat the butter and sugar on medium speed until creamy. Add the egg and beat until incorporated. Add the orange juice and vanilla and beat until combined.

3. On low speed, slowly add the flour mixture, scraping down the sides of the bowl and paddle as needed. Continue beating until smooth.

4. Form the dough into two discs and wrap each in plastic wrap. Chill the dough for at least 2 hours.

5. Remove one disc from the refrigerator and roll it out on a lightly floured surface until it is ⅛-inch thick.

6. Using a 3½-inch-diameter cookie cutter, cut circles out of the dough. Transfer them to a tray, with plastic wrap between the layers, and refrigerate. Roll out the second half of the dough and repeat the cutting and chilling steps above.

7. Position two racks in the top and bottom thirds of the oven and preheat the oven to 350 degrees. Line two baking sheets with parchment paper.

8. Working with sixteen circles at a time, while keeping the rest of the dough chilled, place 1 teaspoon of the fruit filling in the center of each circle. Fold the circle up at the bottom and inward at both sides, forming a triangle, leaving about a ½-inch opening in the center. Chill the shaped cookies for at least 15 minutes before baking.

9. Bake for 8 minutes, then rotate the baking sheets front to back and top to bottom. Bake an additional 6 minutes. The edges of the cookies should be lightly browned in contrast to the pale center.

10. Remove from the oven and slide the parchment paper off the baking sheet onto a wire rack to cool completely. Repeat baking remaining cookies as above when baking sheet has cooled.

Fig Filling:
½ CUP PLUS 2 TABLESPOONS ORANGE JUICE
¼ CUP PLUS 1 TABLESPOON LEMON JUICE
1½ CUPS ROUGHLY CHOPPED DRIED FIGS
⅔ CUP RAISINS
¼ CUP SUGAR
⅛ TEASPOON GROUND CINNAMON
½ TEASPOON VANILLA EXTRACT

Cherry Filling:
¼ CUP ORANGE JUICE
3 TABLESPOONS LEMON JUICE
½ TEASPOON ORANGE ZEST
⅛ TEASPOON ALMOND EXTRACT
⅛ TEASPOON GROUND CINNAMON
3 TABLESPOONS SUGAR
2 CUPS DRIED CHERRIES
¾ CUP DRIED CRANBERRIES

Apricot Filling:
¾ CUP ORANGE JUICE
¼ CUP PLUS 1 TABLESPOON LEMON JUICE
2¼ CUPS DRIED APRICOTS
¼ CUP PLUS 1 TABLESPOON SUGAR

1. Combine all the ingredients plus 1 tablespoon of water in a medium saucepan. Simmer over medium-low heat for about 2? minutes, until the dried fruit softens and the liquid is reduced by about half. Remove it from the heat and let cool.

2. Place the cooled mixture in a food processor fitted with the blade attachment and process until a smooth jam is formed.

HAZELNUT SANDWICH COOKIES

These decadent cookies are a hazelnut-lover's dream. A friend schedules a quiet moment of solitude (cookie alone time) in which to savor each bite. The filling is a gianduja ganache (pronounced *john-DOO-yah*). Gianduja is a smooth and creamy hazelnut milk chocolate available at specialty food stores or online (see Sources page 175). *MAKES 34 SANDWICH COOKIES*

For the cookies:

3 ⅛ CUPS ALL-PURPOSE FLOUR

1 ¾ CUPS HAZELNUTS, TOASTED, SKINNED, AND FINELY GROUND (SEE INSTRUCTIONS ON PAGE 000)

¾ TEASPOON SALT

1 CUP (2 STICKS) UNSALTED BUTTER, ROOM TEMPERATURE

¾ CUP PLUS 1 TABLESPOON SUGAR

2 EGGS, ROOM TEMPERATURE

1 TEASPOON VANILLA EXTRACT

For the gianduja filling:

1 ¾ CUPS FINELY CHOPPED GIANDUJA

⅓ CUP HALF-AND-HALF

½ CUP (1 STICK) UNSALTED BUTTER, SOFTENED

For the ganache garnish:

1 HEAPING CUP (6 OUNCES) FINELY CHOPPED BITTERSWEET CHOCOLATE

⅓ CUP PLUS 2 TEASPOONS HALF-AND-HALF

To mix and bake cookies:

1. In a medium bowl, whisk together the flour, hazelnuts, and salt.

2. In the bowl of a stand mixer fitted with the paddle attachment, beat the butter and sugar on medium speed until smooth.

3. Add the eggs one at a time, then the vanilla, to the butter mixture and beat on low speed until incorporated, scraping down the sides of the bowl and the paddle.

4. Add the flour mixture and beat until well combined, scraping down the sides of the bowl and paddle with a rubber spatula or plastic scraper, as needed.

5. Divide the dough into three portions. Form each into a ball, then flatten them into discs and wrap them in plastic wrap. Refrigerate for at least 1 hour or until firm and chilled throughout.

6. Position two racks in the top and bottom thirds of the oven and preheat the oven to 350 degrees. Line two baking sheets with parchment paper.

7. When the dough has chilled, generously flour your work surface. Remove 1 disc from the refrigerator and unwrap. Use a rolling pin to roll the dough to about $\frac{1}{8}$ inch thick. Dust with flour as necessary to keep the dough from sticking to the work surface and the rolling pin.

8. Cut out 3-inch circles with a cookie cutter and place them on the baking sheets using a small offset spatula to carefully lift them up from your work surface.

9. Bake for 6 minutes, then rotate the baking sheets from top to bottom and front to back. Bake an additional 6 to 7 minutes. The cookies should be a deep brown color. Remove from the oven and transfer the cookies to a wire rack until completely cooled.

To make the gianduja filling:

1. Place the chopped gianduja chocolate in a medium, heat-proof bowl.

2. Heat the half-and-half in a small saucepan until it comes to a boil. Pour it over the chocolate and stir until the mixture is smooth. Set aside to cool.

3. When the chocolate mixture is completely cool, whisk in the butter. Place the bowl in the refrigerator and chill for about 5 minutes. Whisk the mixture again and repeat the chilling and whisking until it is thick and creamy. Remove from the refrigerator when the mixture is the consistency of frosting. Set it aside.

To prepare the ganache:

1. Put the chopped bittersweet chocolate in a deep, heat-proof bowl. Bring the half-and-half to a boil in a small saucepan and pour it over the chocolate. Stir together until the mixture is smooth.

To dip, fill, and assemble the cookies:

1. Place a large sheet of wax paper on your work surface. Separate out half of the baked cookies to use as the chocolate garnished tops. Dip each one half way into the ganache, shake gently to remove the excess and place it on the wax paper.

2. Next, spread about 1 tablespoon of the gianduja filling over the bottom side of the remaining cookies using a small offset spatula.

3. When the chocolate ganache has set on the tops, carefully remove the cookies from the wax paper and set them on the filling-topped cookies.

CHOCOLATE SABLÉS

We understand why this has become one of Pierre Hermé's most widely known recipes. The salt magnifies and concentrates the bittersweet chocolate in a way we couldn't imagine until our first transcendent taste. The longer you chill the dough, the easier it will be to slice it and the more likely the sablés will hold their shape during the baking. *MAKES 72 COOKIES*

2¾ CUPS ALL-PURPOSE FLOUR

¾ CUP PLUS 1 TABLESPOON DUTCH-PROCESSED COCOA POWDER

1½ TEASPOONS BAKING SODA

½ TEASPOON SALT

1⅓ CUPS (2⅔ STICKS) UNSALTED BUTTER, ROOM TEMPERATURE

½ CUP GRANULATED SUGAR

1⅔ CUPS PACKED DARK BROWN SUGAR

1 TEASPOON VANILLA EXTRACT

1¾ CUPS BITTERSWEET CHOCOLATE CHUNKS

1. Sift together the flour, cocoa, baking soda, and salt into a large bowl.

2. In the bowl of a stand mixer fitted with the paddle attachment, cream the butter on medium speed until soft and smooth.

3. Add the granulated sugar, brown sugar, and vanilla to the butter. Beat on medium speed until light and fluffy.

4. Add the flour mixture to the butter mixture on low speed and beat just until blended thoroughly.

5. Add the chocolate chunks and mix until they are evenly distributed.

6. Transfer the dough to a work surface. Divide it into six equal pieces and roll each into a 6-inch log. Wrap each log tightly with plastic wrap. Refrigerate the logs until they are firm and chilled, at least 45 minutes. The logs can be refrigerated at this point for up to 3 days or frozen for up to a month (frozen logs should be defrosted before cutting).

7. Position two oven racks in the upper and lower thirds of the oven and preheat the oven to 375 degrees. Line two baking sheets with parchment paper.

8. Remove two logs from the refrigerator and place them on a work surface. With a sharp knife, cut ½-inch-thick slices and place them on the prepared baking sheets spaced 2 inches apart, 12 cookies per baking sheet.

9. Bake for 8 minutes, rotate the baking sheets from front to back and top to bottom, and bake for another 4 minutes or until the centers are just firm to the touch. Remove from the oven, transfer to a wire rack, and cool completely.

10. When the baking sheets have cooled, cut and bake the remaining logs following steps 8 and 9.

LINZER COOKIES

This cookie is based on the classic tart from Linz, Austria. Our cookie version features the ground nuts, cinnamon, and raspberry jam of the original tart. Instead of a lattice crust, a window is stamped out of a top cookie to show the colorful preserves underneath. We make hundreds of heart-shaped linzer cookies for Valentine's Day each year, but a round fluted cutter works well for any celebration. *MAKES 24 SANDWICH COOKIES*

1¼ CUPS PECANS, TOASTED (SEE INSTRUCTIONS ON PAGE 170)

2½ CUPS ALL-PURPOSE FLOUR

1 TEASPOON GROUND CINNAMON

½ TEASPOON SALT

¾ CUP PLUS 2 TABLESPOONS (1¾ STICKS) UNSALTED BUTTER, ROOM TEMPERATURE

¾ CUP SUGAR

2 EGGS, ROOM TEMPERATURE

¾ TEASPOON VANILLA EXTRACT

½ CUP SEEDLESS RASPBERRY JAM

CONFECTIONERS' SUGAR FOR DUSTING

Mixing the cookie dough:

1. Place the pecans in a food processor fitted with a blade attachment. Pulse the machine on and off just until they become a fine meal. (Be careful not to over process or they will turn into a paste.)

2. In a large bowl, combine the ground pecans, flour, cinnamon, and salt, and set aside.

3. In the bowl of a stand mixer fitted with the paddle attachment, beat the butter on medium speed for 1 to 2 minutes, or until smooth and creamy.

4. Add the sugar and continue beating on medium speed until incorporated.

5. On low speed, add the eggs one at a time, beating between additions. Scrape down the sides of the bowl and the paddle as needed and beat until incorporated.

6. Add the vanilla and mix until combined.

7. On low speed, gradually add the flour mixture, stopping the mixer occasionally to scrape down the sides of the bowl and the paddle. Continue mixing until all the ingredients are incorporated, being careful not to over mix.

8. Transfer the dough to a work surface and divide it into four equal pieces. Flatten each piece into a disc shape and wrap each one in plastic wrap. Refrigerate until firm and very cold. The dough can be refrigerated for up to 5 days or frozen for up to a month. (Frozen dough should be defrosted before proceeding.)

Rolling, cutting, and baking:

1. When you're ready to roll out the dough, position two racks in the top and bottom thirds of the oven and preheat the oven to 375 degrees. Line two baking sheets with parchment paper.

2. You will use two discs for bottom cookies and two discs for the top "windowed" cookies. Working with one disc at a time, remove it from the refrigerator, unwrap, and place it on a lightly floured work surface or silicone mat.

3. With a rolling pin, roll the disc into a sheet about ⅛-inch-thick. Using a 2½-inch fluted round cookie cutter, cut out as many pieces as possible and place them on the prepared sheet pan, evenly spaced, and at least ½ inch apart. When making the tops, cut a small circle out of the center of each cookie using a 1½-inch fluted round cookie cutter and place them on the second prepared sheet pan.

4. Reserve the scraps off to the side of your work surface and when you've finished cutting out all the cookies gently mold the scraps together into a disc shape. Wrap the scrap disc with plastic wrap and refrigerate it until chilled. Follow the directions from the beginning of Step 3.

5. Bake the bottom cookies for 6 minutes then rotate the baking sheets from top to bottom and front to back. Bake an additional 6 minutes or until the centers feel firm and the edges are lightly browned. Bake the top cookies for 5 minutes, rotate the baking sheets from top to bottom and front to back. Bake an additional 4 minutes.

6. Remove from the oven and transfer to a wire rack until completely cooled.

To assemble the cookies:

1. Spread 1 teaspoon of jam on the underside of each bottom cookie.

2. Place the top halves of the cookies on a piece of parchment paper and dust lightly with confectioners' sugar.

3. Place the dusted cookie tops onto the jam-covered bottoms.

MOLASSES SPICE COOKIES

We bake more of these than any other cookie. It's the cookie equivalent of comfort food. Just about everyone has a childhood memory of soft, chewy cookies like these, especially if you grew up in New England like we did. As I've come across similar recipes in many earlier cookbooks, it's obvious that the popularity of this cookie has stood the test of time. This recipe takes a little extra time to chill the dough. The first chilling makes it easier to work with and the second chilling will prevent excessive spreading during baking. A.P. *MAKES 40 COOKIES*

3 CUPS ALL-PURPOSE FLOUR

2 TEASPOONS BAKING SODA

½ TEASPOON SALT

1 TEASPOON GROUND CINNAMON

½ TEASPOON GROUND GINGER

½ TEASPOON GROUND CLOVES

1 EGG, ROOM TEMPERATURE

¼ CUP MOLASSES

1 CUP SUGAR, PLUS MORE FOR TOPPING

1¼ CUPS (2½ STICKS) UNSALTED BUTTER, MELTED AND COOLED

1. In a medium bowl combine the flour, baking soda, salt, cinnamon, ginger, and cloves.

2. In the bowl of a stand mixer fitted with the paddle attachment, combine the egg and the molasses on low speed. Add the sugar and beat on medium speed until combined.

3. Add the melted and cooled butter and beat on low speed until it's thoroughly incorporated. Scrape down the sides of the bowl and paddle as needed.

4. On low speed, add the flour mixture in thirds and mix until incorporated. Stop the mixer and scrape down the bowl and paddle between additions.

5. Place a sheet of plastic wrap on a work surface and place the dough in the center. Flatten the dough into a uniform thickness. Wrap with plastic wrap and place in the refrigerator to chill for 20 to 30 minutes.

6. Remove the dough from the refrigerator and unwrap it. Line a plate with a piece of parchment paper. Roll heaping tablespoons of dough into balls about 1½ inches in diameter and place the cookie balls on the plate. Refrigerate until chilled, at least 1 hour.

7. Position two racks in the top and bottom thirds of the oven and preheat the oven to 350 degrees. Line two baking sheets with parchment paper.

8. To garnish the cookies, place a scoopful of white sugar in a medium bowl. Remove the plate from the refrigerator and, working with six dough balls at a time, toss them in the sugar until they are evenly coated.

9. Transfer the sugared dough balls to the prepared baking sheet, evenly spaced about 2 inches apart. Repeat with the rest of the dough balls.

10. Bake for 8 minutes, then rotate the baking sheets from front to back and top to bottom. Bake an additional 7 minutes. The cookies should be dark golden brown with lighter cracks. They will be a little puffy but will deflate slightly as they cool.

11. Remove from the oven and slide the parchment paper with the cookies onto a wire rack to cool completely.

[*Just about everyone has a childhood memory of soft, chewy cookies like these, especially if you grew up in New England like we did.*]

RUGALACH

In the early morning hours after long overnight shifts at my bakery job in Brookline, Massachusetts, I would treat myself by stopping into one of the many Jewish bakeries that lined our street, buying several of these little treats to nibble on my walk home. Ours come closest to those flaky, golden nuggets of pastry rolled in spicy ground nuts than any I've tasted. Baking just one tray at a time in the upper third of the oven will prevent the bottoms from browning too much, before the rugalach is baked through. A.P. *MAKES 32 RUGALACH*

3¼ CUP ALL-PURPOSE FLOUR

¼ TEASPOON SALT

1½ CUPS (12 OUNCES) CREAM CHEESE, ROOM TEMPERATURE

1½ CUPS (3 STICKS) UNSALTED BUTTER, ROOM TEMPERATURE

2¼ TEASPOON VANILLA EXTRACT

2¼ CUPS WALNUT HALVES

2 CUPS SUGAR

1 TABLESPOON PLUS 1 TEASPOON GROUND CINNAMON

To make the dough:

1. In a medium bowl, whisk together the flour and salt.

2. In the bowl of a stand mixer, fitted with the paddle attachment, beat the cream cheese and butter on medium-high speed until smooth. Add the vanilla and mix until incorporated.

3. Reduce the mixer speed to low and add the flour mixture in two stages, beating until a soft dough forms.

4. Transfer the dough to a lightly floured work surface and press it into a rectangle measuring about 8 x 12 inches.

5. Wrap the dough in plastic wrap and chill it for at least 1 hour before rolling it out.

To make the walnut filling:

1. Place the walnuts in a food processor with a blade attachment. Pulse the machine on and off until they are very finely chopped. Combine the walnuts with the sugar and cinnamon and set aside.

To roll and shape:

1. Line two rimmed baking sheets with parchment paper.

2. Remove the dough from the refrigerator and place it on a lightly floured work surface. Divide it lengthwise into two equal pieces. Re-wrap one piece and return it to the refrigerator. Use a rolling pin to roll the dough out into a rectangle measuring 8 inches wide by 14 inches long. Set the dough aside to prepare the work surface for shaping the rugalach.

3. Spread 1 cup of the nut filling on the work surface, covering about the same area as the dough sheet. Place the dough sheet on top of the nut filling and spread another cup of the filling on top of the dough.

4. Using a rolling pin, roll the dough to 11 inches wide by 26 inches long and about ⅛ inch thick. The nut filling will be pressed into both sides of the dough as you roll it out. Gather up any loose nut filling from around the edges of the dough and sprinkle it over the top.

5. Roll up the dough starting from the long edge closest to you, forming a firm but not too tightly shaped log. Be sure the seam is centered on the bottom of the roll.

6. With a sharp knife, cut the log into sixteen pieces that are about 1½ inches wide. Transfer the pieces to a baking sheet, evenly spaced, and refrigerate for at least 20 minutes.

7. Collect any leftover nut filling into the center on the table, add another cup of the nut filling, and repeat the process for the second piece of dough.

To bake the rugalach:

1. Position a rack in the top third of the oven and preheat the oven to 350 degrees while the rugalach is chilling. Remove one baking sheet from the refrigerator and bake for 32 to 35 minutes, rotating the baking sheet halfway through the baking time. They should be firm, lightly browned, and fully baked throughout.

2. Remove from the oven and set the baking sheet on a wire rack to cool for a few minutes. When cool enough to handle, transfer the rugalach from the baking sheet to the rack to cool completely.

3. Bake the second baking sheet as directed in steps 1 and 2.

SWEET & SAVORY SNACKS

As pastry bakers surrounded by rich, buttery pastries all day, we long for salty, crunchy, and savory snacks. This section contains recipes that we've developed using ingredients on hand in the bakery, like nuts, seeds, cheeses, and savory spices, combined in new and novel ways. For example, by adding non-traditional ingredients to a basic shortbread dough, we've created a savory, crumbly cracker that is a satisfying snack.

Most of these recipes require very little effort but will reward you with a versatile, homemade treat that when served to friends often become the topic of conversation. Pecans and almonds that usually serve as a background flavor or garnish in our pastries, become the main attraction in these recipes, as crunchy tidbits that make the perfect nibble alongside a glass of wine, beer, or cocktails.

Some evenings when we aren't up for preparing a meal, we might bring home some Fennel Pepper Crackers and Spiced Pecans, to nosh on alongside small plates of cured meats, cheeses and roasted vegetables. Paired with a glass of wine, it's one of our favorite ways to dine.

ALLAGASH TARALLI

Taralli are a crunchy Italian snack traditionally made with wine. We make ours using Allagash White, a Belgian-style wheat beer from our local brewery, Allagash Brewing Company. Its light crisp flavor is a perfect match for fruity extra virgin olive oil and spices. Feel free to experiment with your own favorite ale. They are rather time consuming, but worth all the effort! As a substitute for type "00" flour, you can use one part pastry flour to three parts all-purpose flour.

Italian flours are classified by their mineral or ash content, unlike North American flours that are categorized by their strength and protein content. Type "00" has the lowest ash content so it is the lightest and silkiest of the Italian flours. If you can't find Italian type "00" flour in your local markets, it can be ordered from King Arthur Flour (called Italian-style flour) listed in Sources (page 175). *MAKES ABOUT 48 TARALLI*

2¾ CUPS TYPE "00" FLOUR

3 CUPS ALL-PURPOSE FLOUR

1 TABLESPOON PLUS 1 TEASPOON KOSHER SALT, PLUS EXTRA FOR GARNISH

1 TABLESPOON PLUS 1 TEASPOON SUGAR

1 TABLESPOON PLUS 1 TEASPOON DRIED OREGANO

2½ TEASPOONS CRUSHED RED PEPPER FLAKES

1¼ CUPS EXTRA VIRGIN OLIVE OIL

12-OUNCE BOTTLE ALLAGASH WHITE BEER (OR ALE OF CHOICE)

1. Line a baking sheet with parchment paper.

2. In the bowl of a stand mixer fitted with the dough hook, place the type "00" flour, all-purpose flour, salt, sugar, oregano, and red pepper flakes and mix together on low speed until incorporated.

3. Add the olive oil and beer and mix on medium speed for about 5 minutes to form a moist dough.

4. Transfer the dough to the baking sheet and form into a rectangle 12 inches by 15 inches. Cover with plastic wrap and refrigerate for at least 2 hours or overnight.

5. When you are ready to shape the taralli, line two baking sheets with parchment paper and set them aside. Position racks in the top and bottom thirds of the oven and preheat the oven to 350 degrees. Fill a large shallow pot with water and slowly bring it to a boil while shaping the taralli.

6. Remove the dough from the refrigerator. Leave the dough on the tray or flip it out onto a cutting board. Using a pizza wheel or a knife, cut the long side into ¾-inch strips. Next, cut the strips into 3 rows of 4-inch pieces.

7. Take each piece and roll it into a rope about 7 inches long. Shape the rope into a ring, making a small knot at the top. Set the rings on the baking sheets as you shape them.

8. Drop the rings into the boiling water, about 7 or 8 at a time. The water should remain at a simmer. When the taralli float to the surface, gently scoop them out of the water with a slotted spoon or a skimmer, allowing them to drain for a moment in the spoon, before placing them back on the baking sheet. You do not have to space the taralli too far apart, as they won't spread while baking. Sprinkle them lightly with kosher salt.

9. Bake for about 20 minutes, then rotate the baking sheets from front to back and top to bottom and bake for 20 minutes longer, until they are a nice, even golden brown. Remove them from the oven and transfer to a wire rack to cool completely.

CANDIED HAZELNUTS

A thin shell of caramelized sugar surrounds a toasted hazelnut in salty-sweet sublimity. These golden candies are the perfect garnish on tarts or cakes —if you can manage not to eat them all first! *MAKES ½ CUP CANDIED HAZELNUTS*

½ CUP HAZELNUTS
1 TABLESPOON LIGHT CORN SYRUP
1½ TEASPOONS SUGAR
¼ TEASPOON SALT

1. Position a rack in the center of the oven and preheat the oven to 350 degrees. Line a baking sheet with parchment paper and lightly spray it with nonstick cooking spray.

2. In a small bowl, combine the hazelnuts, corn syrup, sugar, and salt. Stir well to coat the hazelnuts evenly in the sugar mixture.

3. Spread the nuts out on the baking sheet. Bake for 10 minutes. Then, stirring every few minutes with a heatproof spatula or spoon, bake for an additional 5 to 10 minutes. The sugar coating on the hazelnuts should be a deep amber color and smell like caramel.

4. Place the tray on a wire rack and quickly separate the nuts from each other by spreading them out on the tray with your spatula or spoon. Let cool completely.

SPICED PECANS

This is one of the handiest treats to have around in your kitchen—they can be served on their own with cocktails, crumbled as a dessert topping over fresh fruit compote or ice cream, or paired with cheeses and dessert wine. Any nut or combination of nuts can be substituted for the pecans. Lightly toasting the nuts will heighten their flavor, but you could skip that step if pressed for time.

Note: Nuts should be kept at cool room temperature to prevent the oils from turning rancid and always tasted for freshness before using. *MAKES 2 CUPS SPICED PECANS*

⅔ CUP SUGAR

½ TEASPOON GROUND CINNAMON

½ TEASPOON GROUND GINGER

¼ TEASPOON FRESHLY GRATED NUTMEG

¼ TEASPOON SALT

2 CUPS PECAN HALVES, TOASTED (SEE INSTRUCTIONS ON PAGE 170)

1. Line a baking sheet with parchment paper.

2. Combine the sugar, cinnamon, ginger, nutmeg, salt, and ¼ cup of water in a medium saucepan over medium heat.

3. When the sugar mixture comes to a boil, add the pecans.

4. Stir continuously with a wooden spoon until the mixture thickens and the sugar crystallizes. The nuts should have an opaque sugar coating.

5. Turn the pecans out onto the prepared pan. Stir and spread the nuts to separate them. Let sit until cool.

CHEDDAR SESAME SHORTBREAD

These savory indulgences are crisp on the outside, tender on the inside, buttery, and packed with cheddar. The cayenne pepper gives them a little spicy kick and the sesame seeds add a nice toasty crunch. *MAKES 50 SHORTBREAD*

2 CUPS ALL-PURPOSE FLOUR

¾ TEASPOON SALT

¼ TEASPOON CAYENNE PEPPER

¼ TEASPOON COARSELY GROUND BLACK PEPPER

1 CUP (2 STICKS) UNSALTED BUTTER, ROOM TEMPERATURE

3 CUPS (8 OUNCES) SHREDDED SHARP WHITE CHEDDAR CHEESE, LOOSELY PACKED

1 EGG

¼ CUP SESAME SEEDS, FOR COATING

1. In a medium bowl, sift together the flour, salt, cayenne pepper, and black pepper.

2. In the bowl of a stand mixer fitted with the paddle attachment, beat the butter on medium-high speed until soft and smooth. Add the cheese and gently mix together until just combined.

3. Beat in the egg on low speed, scraping down the bowl and the paddle as needed.

4. Add the flour mixture and mix until it's evenly moistened.

5. On a lightly floured surface, divide the dough into two equal portions and roll each piece into a log approximately 6 inches long with a diameter of 1½ inches. Wrap the logs in plastic wrap and refrigerate overnight.

6. To bake the shortbread, position racks in the top and bottom thirds of the oven and preheat the oven to 400 degrees. Line two baking sheets with parchment paper.

7. Remove one log from the refrigerator, unwrap it, and place it on a cutting board. Cut the log into ¼-inch-thick slices with a sharp knife. Place the sesame seeds in a small bowl. Press a cut side of each slice into the sesame seeds. Place on the baking sheets, seeded side up, evenly spaced, about sixteen to a tray. Rewrap any portion of the log not being baked immediately and refrigerate.

8. Bake the shortbread for 15 minutes, then rotate the baking sheets from front to back and top to bottom and bake for 10 minutes longer. They should be golden around the edges, with lightly browned speckles of cheese on the tops.

9. Slide the parchment off the baking sheet onto a wire rack. Cool the sheet pans before baking the next round of shortbread.

FENNEL PEPPER CRACKERS

These crackers are so fragrant, when they are in the oven we all circle around, breathing deeply. Toasty semolina, fruity olive oil, aromatic fennel seed...you can hear customers asking, "What do you have in the oven?" Most of the time the bakery is filled with a progression of sweet scents: cinnamon, molasses, chocolate, and apples. These crackers are a sensory contrast that we all enjoy. These are crisp, savory treats that are perfect served with your usual cracker accompaniments, but delicate enough to enjoy on their own. *MAKES 76 CRACKERS*

3 CUPS ALL-PURPOSE FLOUR

¼ CUP SEMOLINA

½ TEASPOON INSTANT YEAST

1 TEASPOON COARSELY GROUND BLACK PEPPER

2 TEASPOONS DRIED FENNEL SEED

1 TEASPOON KOSHER SALT PLUS EXTRA FOR SPRINKLING

⅔ CUP WATER, ROOM TEMPERATURE

½ CUP OLIVE OIL

1. Whisk together the flour, semolina, yeast, pepper, fennel, and salt in a large bowl.

2. Pour the water into the bowl of a stand mixer fitted with the hook attachment. Add the flour mixture on low speed, then slowly add the olive oil. Increase the speed to medium and mix until a soft dough comes together. Continue mixing for about 5 minutes or until the surface of the dough is smooth and supple.

3. Shape the dough into a ball and flatten it into a disc. Wrap the disc tightly with plastic wrap and chill for at least 1 hour, or preferably overnight.

4. To shape and bake the crackers, position racks in the top and bottom third of the oven and preheat the oven to 400 degrees. Line two baking sheets with parchment paper.

5. Remove the dough from the refrigerator and divide it in half. Keep one half chilled and place the other half on a lightly floured work surface.

6. Roll the dough into a ¹⁄₁₆-inch thick rectangle with a rolling pin, using flour as necessary to prevent the dough from sticking to the work surface and rolling pin. Allow the rolled dough to rest for about 5 minutes before cutting to prevent it from shrinking back. Before cutting, slide your fingers or a plastic scraper underneath the dough to make sure it isn't stuck to the work surface.

7. Use a dough docker or a fork to pierce the dough evenly over the entire surface. Moisten the surface of the dough with a spray bottle, a pastry brush, or your fingers dipped in water. Sprinkle a small amount of kosher salt evenly over the surface.

8. With a pizza wheel or a sharp knife, cut the dough into 2-inch-wide strips, then cut each strip into a 4-inch-long rectangle. Carefully transfer the pieces to the baking sheets, spacing them evenly about half an inch apart. The trimmings and any scraps can be baked on a separate pan until crisp, or discarded.

9. Bake for 5 minutes, then rotate the baking sheets from top to bottom and front to back. Bake an additional 5 to 7 minutes. They should be golden brown and crisp.

10. Remove the sheets from the oven and slip the parchment paper with the crackers onto a wire rack to cool completely.

> *Toasty semolina, fruity olive oil, aromatic fennel seed... you can hear customers asking, 'What do you have in the oven?'*

FRUIT AND NUT GRANOLA BARS

When we cut the granola bars in the morning we always cut the outside edges off first. The trimmings are placed on a plate on the staff break table. They disappear in minutes! These hearty bars feature many of the nuts, seeds, and dried fruits that are staples in the bakery. Any combination of inclusions can be used as long as the amount of dry ingredients stays the same.

MAKES 30 (1 X 5½-INCH) BARS

1 CUP (2 STICKS) UNSALTED BUTTER

2 CUPS PACKED LIGHT BROWN SUGAR

1½ CUPS PEANUT BUTTER, NATURAL SALTED

1 CUP LIGHT CORN SYRUP

2 TABLESPOONS VANILLA EXTRACT

7 CUPS ROLLED (NOT INSTANT) OATS

ONE 12-OUNCE PACKAGE SMALL CHOCOLATE CHIPS

1½ CUPS DRIED CRANBERRIES

1 CUP HULLED SUNFLOWER SEEDS

½ CUP PUMPKIN SEEDS, TOASTED (SEE INSTRUCTIONS ON PAGE 170)

½ CUP SESAME SEEDS

½ CUP CHOPPED PECANS, TOASTED (SEE INSTRUCTIONS ON PAGE 170)

1. In a small saucepan, melt the butter over low heat and set it aside to cool (it should cool completely before using or it will melt the chocolate chips).

2. Preheat the oven to 375 degrees. Prepare a rimmed 13 x 18-inch baking sheet by lining it with parchment paper and spraying the sides with nonstick cooking spray.

3. In a large bowl, combine the brown sugar, peanut butter, corn syrup, and vanilla.

4. In another large bowl, combine the oats, chocolate, cranberries, sunflower seeds, pumpkin seeds, sesame seeds, and pecans.

5. Add half of the dry ingredients and half of the melted butter to the peanut butter mixture. Mix and knead with your hands to combine.

6. Add the remaining dry ingredients and the rest of the butter and mix until all of the ingredients are thoroughly incorporated.

7. Spread the mixture out onto the prepared baking sheet and press it down to fill the pan. Cover the mixture with another sheet of parchment paper and use a rolling pin to make sure it is pressed firmly to a uniform thickness.

8. Bake for 10 to 11 minutes, rotating the pan halfway through the baking time. The edges will be a light golden brown. The mixture will look under-baked in the center, but will set up after cooling.

9. Transfer the pan to a wire rack and let it cool for several hours before cutting.

10. To cut, run a knife around the outside edge to loosen it from the pan and then flip the pan over onto a cutting board. Using a very sharp knife, cut into any size you like. A ruler and a small paring knife work well to score the top of the granola into strips. Use a large sharp knife to cut straight down through the bars on the score marks.

TRUFFLED ALMONDS

A François Payard recipe inspired us to make these tempting confections that have become the most addictive treat in the bakery. The sugar and chocolate each form their own distinct crunchy layers, while the cocoa adds a velvety finish that melts in your mouth and intensifies the chocolate. Freezing the sugar-coated almonds causes the melted chocolate to harden quickly when stirred in, forming a perfect coating. Mixing in the cocoa powder helps to separate the nuts from each other.

MAKES 2 CUPS TRUFFLED ALMONDS

⅔ CUP SUGAR

½ TEASPOON SALT

2 CUPS WHOLE RAW ALMONDS, TOASTED (SEE INSTRUCTIONS ON PAGE 170)

6 OUNCES BITTERSWEET CHOCOLATE

⅓ CUP DUTCH-PROCESSED COCOA POWDER

1. Line a baking sheet with parchment paper.

2. Combine the sugar, salt, and ¼ cup of water in a medium saucepan over medium heat.

3. When the sugar mixture comes to a boil, add the almonds.

4. With a wooden spoon, stir continuously until the mixture thickens and the sugar crystallizes. The nuts should have an opaque sugar coating.

5. Turn the almonds out on to the prepared pan. Stir and spread the nuts to separate them.

6. When the nuts are cool, transfer them to a medium bowl and place them in the freezer for about half an hour.

7. Melt the chocolate in a medium heat-proof bowl set over a pan of simmering water.

8. Remove the nuts from the freezer and pour the melted chocolate over them. Stir quickly to coat all the almonds evenly.

9. Sprinkle the cocoa powder over the nuts and, using a rubber spatula, lift and toss the nuts to separate them.

10. Place a piece of parchment paper or aluminum foil on a work surface. Transfer the nuts to a colander or fine-mesh sieve placed over the prepared work surface and gently shake off excess cocoa. Gently transfer the truffled nuts to a serving bowl.

> *The sugar and chocolate each form their own distinct crunchy layers, while the cocoa adds a velvety finish that melts in your mouth and intensifies the chocolate.*

BASIC RECIPES

This section contains many of the basic recipes that we have at our disposal every day in the bakery. These are the doughs, fillings, and toppings that we mix and match to create endless combinations, in rhythm with the seasons. The crumb toppings can be substituted for each other in these recipes to create subtle textural changes, or they can be used as a topping for your own favorite muffin and quickbread recipes. If you have any caramel filling leftover, use it to drizzle over warm fruit or ice cream. Or, try our favorite indulgence and add a few drops to your coffee.

CHOCOLATE TART DOUGH

This dark, intensely cocoa-flavored tart dough is beautiful as well as delicious. The dough is easy to work with and exceptionally tender when baked. This dough pairs well with any chocolate or nut-based fillings. To maintain the dark chocolate color, brush off any flour you have used while rolling out the dough before lining the tart rings. *MAKES ONE 9-INCH TART OR SIX 4-INCH TARTELETTES*

⅓ CUP PLUS 1 TABLESPOON CONFECTIONERS' SUGAR

¼ CUP PLUS 1 TABLESPOON DUTCH-PROCESSED COCOA POWDER

1 CUP ALL-PURPOSE FLOUR

4 TABLESPOONS UNSALTED BUTTER, CUBED AND CHILLED

1 EGG YOLK

1 TABLESPOON PLUS 2 TEASPOONS HEAVY CREAM

To make the dough:

1. Over a large bowl, using a fine mesh sieve, sift the confectioners' sugar, cocoa, and flour.

2. In the bowl of a stand mixer fitted with the paddle attachment, combine the flour mixture and cubed butter until the butter is reduced to pea-size pieces.

3. Add the yolk and the heavy cream and continue to mix until the dough roughly comes together. It will look extremely dry at first, but will form a crumbly, yet moist dough.

4. Press the dough into a ball, flatten it slightly into a disc, and wrap it tightly with plastic wrap. Place the dough in the refrigerator to rest for at least 1 hour before using.

5. Freeze any dough that isn't going to be used in the next day or two. About 30 minutes before you are ready to roll out the tart shell, remove the dough from the refrigerator.

To line a 9-inch tart ring:

1. Place the dough disc on a lightly floured work surface. Roll it out into a circle, starting from the center of the disc and rolling outward towards all sides, lifting the dough and giving it a quarter turn occasionally to keep it from sticking to the work surface.

2. Roll the dough into a circle about ⅛ inch thick and 11 inches in diameter (or 2 inches larger than the diameter of your tart pan). If the dough has warmed and become difficult to work with, place it in the refrigerator for a few minutes to firm up before continuing.

3. Carefully press the dough into a 9-inch tart ring without stretching it. Use a sharp knife to trim any excess around the rim. Place the shell in the refrigerator for at least 15 minutes to chill.

To line and bake 4-inch tartelettes

1. Position a rack in the center of the oven and preheat the oven to 375 degrees. Line a baking sheet with parchment paper. Position a rack in the center of the oven.

2. Place the dough disc on a lightly floured work surface. Roll the dough, starting from the center of the disc and rolling outward towards all sides, lifting the dough and giving it a quarter turn occasionally to keep it from sticking to the work surface.

3. Roll the dough to ⅛ inch thick and cut out circles using a 4½-inch cookie cutter. If the dough has warmed and become difficult to work with, place it in the refrigerator for a few minutes to firm up before continuing.

4. Carefully press the dough into your 4-inch tart pans without stretching it. Use a sharp knife to trim any excess around the rim. Place the formed shells in the refrigerator for at least 15 minutes to chill.

5. Remove the formed shells from the refrigerator and place them on the baking sheet. Use a fork to pierce the bottom of each tart shell. Cut parchment paper into 6-inch squares and press it over the tart dough. Fill to the very top with dried beans.

6. Bake for 15 minutes. Carefully lift out the parchment paper and beans from the tart shells. Bake an additional 10 to 12 minutes. The tart dough should be firm on the bottom and the edges crisp. Place the shells on a wire rack to cool in the tin.

PERFECT TART DOUGH

This recipe is a gift to the world from Pierre Hermé. We added a bit of cake flour to make it more tender. The dough is so easy to make—almost like making a cookie dough—but the result is a crust that is exceptionally delicate and flaky. It is easy to work with, but requires resting time, so plan accordingly. This remarkably versatile dough can be used for just about any fruit, cream, or savory fillings. *MAKES TWELVE 3-INCH TARTELETTES OR TWO 9-INCH TARTS*

1½ CUPS ALL-PURPOSE FLOUR

¼ CUP CAKE FLOUR

½ TEASPOON SALT

13 TABLESPOONS (1⅔ STICKS) UNSALTED BUTTER, SOFTENED

3 TABLESPOONS WHOLE MILK, ROOM TEMPERATURE

1 EGG YOLK, ROOM TEMPERATURE

½ TEASPOON SUGAR

Making the dough:

1. In a medium bowl, whisk together the all-purpose flour, cake flour, and salt.

2. In the bowl of a stand mixer fitted with the paddle attachment, beat the butter on medium speed until it is smooth and creamy.

3. Reduce to low speed and add the milk, egg yolk, and sugar. Beat until the mixture is blended. At this stage, it will look curdled.

4. Add the flour mixture in small increments, mixing until a soft dough forms.

5. Divide the dough into two equal portions. Shape each portion into a ball and flatten each into a disc. Wrap the discs tightly with plastic wrap and chill for at least 4 hours or overnight.

To line a 9-inch tart ring

1. Place the tart ring or a tart pan with a removable bottom on a baking sheet lined with parchment paper.

2. Remove a dough disc from the refrigerator and place it on a lightly floured work surface. Starting from the center, with a rolling pin, roll out toward the edges, lifting the dough and giving it an occasional quarter turn to keep it from sticking to the work surface.

3. Roll the dough into a circle, about ⅛ inch thick and 11 inches in diameter (or 2 inches larger than the diameter of your tart pan). If the dough has warmed and become difficult to work with, place it in the refrigerator for a few minutes to firm up before continuing.

4. Carefully press the dough into the ring or pan without stretching it. Use a sharp knife to trim any excess around the rim. Place the shell in the refrigerator for at least 1 hour to chill, or overnight.

To partially bake a 9-inch tart shell:

1. Position a rack in the bottom third of the oven and preheat the oven to 425 degrees. Pierce the bottom of the tart shell with a fork a few times, then line the inside of the tart shell with parchment paper or aluminum foil. Fill it to the top with dried beans. Bake for 15 minutes.

2. Carefully lift out the parchment paper and beans. Return the tart shell to the oven for another 5 minutes. Rotate the pan and pierce any bubbles that have formed in the bottom of the shell. Bake for another 10 minutes. Remove the pan from the oven and cool on a wire rack.

SWEET TART DOUGH

One of our favorite and most versatile pastry doughs in the bakery. Similar in consistency to shortbread, the confectioners' sugar creates the most tender crumb. If it warms up and becomes soft while you are working, return it to the refrigerator to chill for a few minutes. You can patch any holes or thin spots without worry—its fine texture won't be affected. We like the crumbly texture of this dough combined with cream or curd based fillings. *MAKES THREE 9-INCH TARTS*

½ CUP ALMOND MEAL

¼ TEASPOON SALT

2¾ CUPS ALL-PURPOSE FLOUR

¼ TEASPOON VANILLA EXTRACT

1 EGG PLUS 1 YOLK, ROOM TEMPERATURE

14 TABLESPOONS (1¼ STICKS) UNSALTED BUTTER, ROOM TEMPERATURE

1 CUP CONFECTIONERS' SUGAR, SIFTED

Making the dough:

1. In a medium bowl, whisk together the almond meal, salt, and all-purpose flour.

2. In a small bowl, using a fork, stir together the vanilla, egg, and yolk.

3. In the bowl of a stand mixer fitted with the paddle attachment, beat the butter and confectioners' sugar on medium speed until the mixture is smooth and creamy.

4. Add the egg mixture on low speed and beat until it is incorporated. Gradually add the flour mixture. Scrape down the sides of the bowl and paddle and continue to beat until all the ingredients are thoroughly incorporated.

5. Transfer the dough to a work surface and divide it into three equal pieces. Gently shape each piece into a ball, flatten them slightly into discs, and wrap them tightly with plastic wrap.

6. Place the dough in the refrigerator to rest for at least 1 hour or overnight. About 30 minutes before you are ready to roll out the tart shell, remove the dough from the refrigerator.

To line a tart ring:

Follow instructions for Perfect Tart Dough (page 158)

To partially bake a 9-inch tart shell:

Follow baking instructions for Perfect Tart Dough (page 158)

RUSTIC TART DOUGH

One of our flakiest pastry doughs, we use it for hand-formed galettes, called Rustic Tarts, in the bakery, but it would work just as well in a traditional tart ring or as a pie dough. The discs or rolled-out rounds can be stored in the refrigerator, wrapped tightly with plastic wrap for up to 3 days or frozen for up to 2 weeks. To use the frozen dough, transfer it to the refrigerator to defrost the night before you plan to make your tart. *MAKES ONE 8-INCH TART OR FOUR 4-INCH TARTS*

1 CUP PLUS 1 TEASPOON ALL-PURPOSE FLOUR

½ TEASPOON SALT

⅛ TEASPOON BAKING POWDER

6 TABLESPOONS UNSALTED BUTTER, CUBED AND CHILLED

⅓ CUP CREAM CHEESE, CUBED AND CHILLED

1 TABLESPOON PLUS 1 TEASPOON ICE COLD WATER

Making the dough:

1. In a large bowl, whisk together the flour, salt, and baking powder. With your fingertips or a pastry cutter, blend the butter into the dry ingredients until it's reduced to pea-size chunks.

2. Add the cream cheese to the flour mixture and blend it in with your fingertips until the mixture has the consistency of a coarse meal. Add the water to the mixture and using a fork or your fingertips, gently toss all of the ingredients together until most of the dry particles are moistened. It will look crumbly and not quite hold together at this point.

3. Carefully form the dough mixture into a loose ball and gently flatten it into a disc. If making small tarts, divide the dough into four equal portions, then form them into discs. Wrap the discs in plastic wrap and place them in the refrigerator to chill and rest for at least an hour or overnight.

To roll out the dough:

1. Place the dough disc on a lightly floured work surface. Starting from the center of the disc, using a rolling pin, roll outward toward the edges, lifting the dough and giving it a quarter turn occasionally to keep it from sticking to the work surface.

2. Roll the dough into a circle about ⅛ inch thick. For a large hand-formed tart, roll it out to 11 inches in diameter, for a small tart about 7 inches in diameter. If the dough has warmed and becomes difficult to work with, place it in the refrigerator for a few minutes to firm up before continuing.

3. Place the rolled out dough on a baking sheet lined with parchment paper, cover it with plastic wrap, and transfer to the refrigerator for at least 1 hour to chill.

PASTRY POINTERS

There are no secrets to making great pastry, but you'll want to keep in a mind a few tips in order to bake flaky tender pastries every time:

- Bring your ingredients to the correct temperature. If room temperature butter is called for, be sure to plan enough time to remove it from the refrigerator to warm up. If chilled butter or water is called for, the colder the better. You could even place them in the freezer for a few minutes before starting your work to ensure the coldest temperatures possible.

- Minimal mixing and gentle handling are key. Use your fingertips, a pastry cutter, or the paddle attachment in a stand mixer to cut the butter into the flour and work as quickly as you can. Follow the directions in each recipe for chilling and resting the dough. This gives the gluten proteins in the flour time to relax so that the dough won't spring back when you roll it out.

- Be careful not to force or stretch the dough into shape. Stretching creates elasticity that will cause the dough to shrink during baking. If it springs back while you're working with it, just give it a few minutes' rest in the refrigerator before continuing. Do the same thing if the dough warms and becomes sticky while you are rolling it out. After filling the tart ring, every recipe calls for a short rest period in the refrigerator to give the gluten another chance to relax after the workout it's had.

- A technique that we use in the bakery to achieve crisp pastry shells when working with pre-baked crusts: While the tart shell is baking, beat an egg with a pinch of salt. A few minutes before the tart has reached its desired color, remove it from the oven and lightly brush the egg wash on the bottom and sides of the shell. Return it to the oven until the desired color is reached and the egg has set. Let cool before filling.

- For convenience, you can mix these tart doughs ahead of time and store them until you're ready to make your tart. All of our doughs keep very well in the refrigerator for up to 3 days, or frozen in discs or rolled out rounds for up to 3 weeks.

CARAMEL SAUCE

This buttery sweet sauce is an essential component of two of our tart recipes—but the possibilities for its use are endless! Some of our favorites are a drizzle over ice cream, a thin layer on a butter cookie, or a spoonful in coffee or hot apple cider. Nothing is better than the flavors of caramelized sugar, fresh dairy, and a touch of salt. *MAKES ¾ CUP*

¾ CUP SUGAR

2 TABLESPOONS LIGHT CORN SYRUP

3 TABLESPOONS UNSALTED BUTTER

¼ CUP HEAVY CREAM

1 TABLESPOON SOUR CREAM

PINCH SALT

1. Place the sugar, corn syrup, and 1½ teaspoons of water in a small saucepan. Have the butter, cream, and sour cream measured and ready. Cook the sugar over medium heat. Use a pastry brush dipped in water to wash away any sugar crystals stuck to the side of the pan.

2. Cook the sugar until it reaches a medium amber color and immediately remove it from the burner. This happens very quickly after it starts to brown and continues to darken after it is pulled off the heat, so be attentive.

3. Quickly whisk in the butter. The sugar will bubble and might spatter a little.

4. Whisk in the heavy cream and sour cream. The mixture will be smooth and creamy, but somewhat thin. It will thicken as it cools. Add the salt and set it aside to cool.

CREAM CHEESE FILLING

This creamy filling is very subtly flavored with vanilla, almond, and citrus. It has just the right amount of sweetness to complement the tang of the cream cheese. Substitute lemon zest for the orange if you prefer. We use this filling in our Babka and Fruit and Cream Cheese Tarts.

MAKES 1 HEAPING CUP

1 EGG YOLK, ROOM TEMPERATURE
½ TEASPOON VANILLA EXTRACT
¼ TEASPOON ALMOND EXTRACT
¼ TEASPOON ORANGE ZEST
PINCH SALT
1 CUP (8 OUNCES) CREAM CHEESE, ROOM TEMPERATURE
⅛ CUP SUGAR

1. In a small bowl, stir together the egg yolk, vanilla extract, almond extract, orange zest, and salt, using a fork.

2. In a medium bowl, beat together the cream cheese and sugar with a wooden spoon until thoroughly combined. Add the egg mixture and beat until fully incorporated.

3. If making ahead of time, transfer to a covered container and refrigerate until you are ready to use. Bring to room temperature to allow filling to spread easily.

FRANGIPANE

Frangipane is a classic French pastry filling. It is light and cake-like when baked and adds just the right nutty and sweet notes when combined with flaky pastry and fresh fruit. It can be varied by substituting another nut for the traditional almond, we sometimes use walnuts. We use this filling in our Frangipane Tarts (pages 70-73) and Almond Croissants (page 29). *MAKES 1½ CUPS FRANGIPANE*

1 CUP ALMOND MEAL

1 TABLESPOON ALL-PURPOSE FLOUR

PINCH SALT

7 TABLESPOONS UNSALTED BUTTER, SOFTENED

½ CUP SUGAR

1 EGG, ROOM TEMPERATURE

1 TABLESPOON RUM

1 TABLESPOON ALMOND EXTRACT

1. In a small bowl, whisk together the almond meal, all-purpose flour, and salt.

2. In the bowl of a stand mixer fitted with the paddle attachment, beat the butter and sugar on medium speed until well blended.

3. Add the egg, rum, and almond extract and beat until incorporated. Scrape down the sides of the bowl and paddle as needed.

4. Add the flour mixture on low speed. Scrape down the sides of the bowl and paddle and gradually increase to medium speed. Beat until all the ingredients are well incorporated.

5. If not using immediately, transfer the frangipane to a tightly covered storage container and refrigerate for up to 3 days.

BROWN BUTTER STREUSEL

If you are looking for a streusel that is sweet, buttery, spicy, and nutty, this is the one you want. This dark molasses hued topping is a bold, flavorful addition to tarts and cakes. The browned butter adds an extra level of toastiness to this indulgent garnish. *MAKES ABOUT 2 CUPS STREUSEL*

7 TABLESPOONS UNSALTED BUTTER

½ CUP PACKED DARK BROWN SUGAR

¾ CUP ALL-PURPOSE FLOUR

1½ TEASPOONS GROUND CINNAMON

½ CUP SLICED ALMONDS

1. To brown the butter, place it in a small saucepan, melt it over medium heat, and simmer gently.

2. Remove it from the heat when the milk solids on the bottom begin to brown and give off a nutty aroma. Set aside and let it cool to room temperature.

3. In a medium bowl, whisk together the sugar, flour, and cinnamon. Drizzle the butter over the flour mixture, being sure to scrape in all the browned bits from the bottom of the pan. Using a fork, toss together until the dry ingredients are evenly moistened. Stir in the almonds.

4. Transfer to a covered container and refrigerate. The streusel can be stored in the refrigerator for up to one week or in the freezer for up to 3 weeks.

STREUSEL

Streusel is a crumbly topping made of few ingredients—flour, sugar, salt, and butter. How can such a simple concoction add so much to the cakes, tarts, and pastries it adorns? This component recipe is a good example of how wonderful ingredients are when brought simply together in an uncomplicated way. *MAKES ABOUT 2 CUPS STREUSEL*

¼ CUP GRANULATED SUGAR

¼ CUP PACKED DARK BROWN SUGAR

⅛ TEASPOON SALT

1½ CUPS ALL-PURPOSE FLOUR

7 TABLESPOONS UNSALTED BUTTER, MELTED AND COOLED

1. In a large bowl, whisk together the granulated sugar, brown sugar, salt, and flour.

2. Add the butter. Blend it into the flour mixture using your fingers or a pastry blender until it's evenly moistened and resembles coarse crumbs.

3. Can be used immediately or transferred to a tightly covered storage container and kept refrigerated until ready to use. The streusel can be stored in the refrigerator for up to 3 days or in the freezer for up to 3 weeks.

TOASTED NUTS

Follow these directions when a recipe calls for toasted nuts.

1. Preheat the oven to 350 degrees.

2. Spread the nuts in a single layer on a baking sheet and bake for 8 to 12 minutes, stirring once or twice to evenly toast. The nuts will darken in color and give off a toasted aroma. Watch carefully as they can burn quickly.

3. To skin hazelnuts, place the toasted nuts into a clean towel, bring the corners together to bundle it up, and rub the nuts vigorously against each other inside the towel, until most of the skin comes off.

POACHED PEARS

Poaching pears enhances their subtle sweet flavor and makes them more tender. Choose ripe but firm fruit, the flesh giving gently when pressed. *MAKES 4 POACHED PEARS*

4 LARGE PEARS, RIPE TO SEMI-RIPE (BARTLETT, BOSC, OR ANJOU), PEELED, CORED, AND CUT IN HALF
1 CUP SUGAR
¼ CUP LEMON JUICE
ONE (2-INCH) PIECE OF VANILLA BEAN, SPLIT IN HALF LENGTHWISE

1. Bring 4 cups of water and the sugar to a boil in a heavy, non-reactive pot.

2. Reduce the heat and lower to a simmer. Add the lemon juice, vanilla bean, and pear halves. Place a circle of parchment paper directly on top of the pears to keep them from browning.

3. Cook the pears at a low simmer for 15 to 40 minutes depending on their ripeness. You can press down on the parchment paper occasionally to keep the fruit submerged so that it cooks evenly. Add more water to cover the fruit, if needed .

4. Test a pear by inserting a paring knife into its thickest part. It should be tender, but you should still feel a slight resistance.

5. Remove from the heat and cool the pears in the syrup. If they are overdone, strain and cool the fruit separately.

6. Store the fruit in the syrup overnight in the refrigerator before using. The fruit can be stored for up to 3 days in the syrup in a tightly covered container.

7. When using the fruit in a tart, the strained syrup can be reduced to make a glaze for the tart. To make a glaze with the syrup while the tart is baking, place the syrup in a non-reactive saucepan and cook over medium heat until it is reduced to a thick syrup. Remove from the heat and let it cool slightly before brushing it on the warm tart.

HEARTFELT THANKS TO ALL!

A life lesson that I've taken from this experience is that one does not write a book alone, and I cannot say enough for all of those people who have made this project possible. ¶ My thanks to Tara Smith, for her enthusiasm and willingness to go the extra mile, both in working on this book and every day in the bakery. ¶ To all of our wonderful bakery staff who have allowed me the time to focus on the writing of this book. Without their talent, skill, and dedication, the bakery could never run as smoothly as it does. ¶ I am most beholden to Sara Deane, our bakery manager, who handles daily crises with equanimity, and our production manager, Tim Gosnell, who keeps everyone on task and in good spirits. ¶ I owe a special thanks to our editor Kathleen Fleury, who proposed the idea of writing a bakery cookbook. For guiding us through the process, before, during, and long after giving birth to her first child, Ella. For her great faith and confidence, and for being so remarkably open to all of our ideas, I am truly grateful. ¶ A huge thank you to Miroslaw Jurek at Down East who is responsible for making this the beautiful book it is. ¶ We were incredibly fortunate to work with such a gifted photographer as Sean Alonzo Harris, who so patiently fielded questions and ideas from at least one photography amateur during our photo shoots. ¶ I'm also grateful to Martha Fenton, for both her remarkable talent in finding order in my own writing and her cool readiness to meet any deadline.¶ To the master bakers and instructors who have guided and inspired me, including Didier Rosada, Philippe LeCorre, Jeffrey Hamelman, Craig Ponsford, among others, for so generously sharing their knowledge with me and with scores of other professional/aspiring bakers, I am deeply grateful.¶ Thank you to Dan Edson, who generously contributed his time and considerable expertise as an editor, baker, and croissant tester.¶ I wish to thank Abe Faber and Christy Timon for their consummate passion and professionalism as they showed me the finer points of baking. To so many bakers, Clear Flour Bread remains the quintessential neighborhood bakery.¶ To our friends and business partners, Victor Leon and Dana Street, for taking a leap of faith and opening Standard Baking Co. with us seventeen years ago.¶ A special thanks and appreciation to our wonderful customers—both local regulars and seasonal visitors who have been so kind and supportive of us for seventeen years—they make the long hours worthwhile.¶ From the beginning, my lovely friends Kate Pullano and Jane Newkirk not only encouraged my pursuit of baking, but so kindly understood whenever my need for sleep took precedence over socializing and holiday gatherings.¶ Above all, my husband Matt, who encouraged my sudden fascination with baking over twenty years ago. For helping in every way possible on this book while working countless hours running the bakery. Without his gentle love and support (not to mention home-cooked meals), Standard Baking Co., and this book, would never exist.

Alison

I have many people to thank for supporting me in my life and career. First and foremost, thanks to my family for the encouragement and endless enthusiasm for all my endeavors.¶ Thanks to Matt James and Alison Pray for deciding I was a good fit for the bakery, and for all their trust in my work. I am honored to be partnered with Alison on this incredible project.¶ I owe a debt of gratitude to all of the chefs from both the Culinary Institute of America, and Jeffrey Hamelman and the crew at King Arthur Flour. They very graciously passed on their knowledge, skills, and philosophies during my formal education.¶ I greatly appreciate all of the tasting done by my co-workers, friends, and neighbors, who were not permitted to be on diets throughout this process. I would most especially like to thank my husband Christopher, who fearlessly risks my crabbiness with his honest critiques. His thoughtful evaluations inspire me to never settle, his ideas and contributions lead to entertaining collaborations, and creating his next favorite treat is my greatest ambition. Without his love and humor, talented editing, and tireless attention—not to mention the continuous dishwashing—this project would not have been realized. My heartfelt thanks to all!

Tara

INDEX

SOURCES

For ingredients or supplies that aren't available in your area, contact the following suppliers:

The Baker's Catalogue
King Arthur Flour
P.O. Box 876, Norwich, VT 05055
800-827-6836, kingarthurflour.com
Baking and pastry tools and equipment, specialty flours, vanilla beans, and other specialty ingredients.

Bridge Kitchenware
17 Waverly Place, Madison, NJ 07940
973-377-3900, bridgekitchenware.com
Kitchen tools and bakeware.

Chicago Metallic Bakeware
300 Knightsbridge Parkway Suite 500, Lincolnshire, IL 60069. 1-800-238-Bake, chicagometallicbakeware.com
Specialty bakeware manufacturer including mini-popover pans.

J.B. Prince Company
36 East 31st St., New York, NY 10016, 800-473-0577, jbprince.com
Baking and pastry tools and equipment.

Kerekes Bakery & Resturant Equipment
6103 15th Ave., Brooklyn, NY 11219, 800-525-5556, BakeDeco.com
Specialty baking molds, including stainless-steel cake rings, timbale molds, and baba cups.

LeRoux Kitchen
161 Commercial St., Portland, ME 04101, 207-553-7665, lerouxkitchen.com
Bakeware, equipment, tools, and specialty ingredients.

Vermont Butter & Cheese Creamery
P.O. Box 95, Websterville, VT 05678, 1-800-884-6287, vermontcreamery.com
Artisanal dairy products, including cultured, high-butterfat butter. Available at many regional specialty food stores. On-line mail order available through their website.

Williams-Sonoma, Inc.
3250 Van Ness Ave., San Francisco, CA 94109, 877-812-6235, williams-sonoma.com
Kitchen equipment, bakeware, and tools.

World Wide Chocolate
643 Franklin Pierce Hwy., Barrington, NH 03825, 1-800-664-9410, worldwidechocolate.com
Imported gourmet chocolate from around the world.